THE COMPLETE GUIDE TO
WORLD WAR II

An Imprint of Sterling Publishing
1166 Avenue of The Americas
New York, NY, 10036

ISBN: 978-1-4351-6170-2

Manufactured in China
Lot #:
2 4 6 8 10 9 8 7 5 3 1
08/15

Picture Credits
(Key: t=top, b=bottom, l=left, r=right, c=center)

Maps by: Meridian Mapping.

THE COMPLETE GUIDE TO
WORLD WAR II

RICHARD PANCHYK and SIMON ADAMS

Sandy Creek
NEW YORK

CONTENTS

Words in **bold** are explained in the Glossary on page 142.

INTRODUCTION

World War II was the most costly war in human history. More people died in this war than in any war ever fought before. It affected both the armed services fighting abroad and civilians at home. It was a truly global war, fought on five continents. Soldiers traveled across the world to fight, and planes flew hundreds of miles to bomb the enemy.

The World at Arms

It is estimated that 100 million men fought during World War II. About one quarter—22 million—of them died. The total cost in pay, arms, equipment, medical care, and other items necessary to keep the men fighting is unknown, but it runs into the billions of dollars.

Sailors abandon the burning USS California after the attack on Pearl Harbor in 1941.

FAST FACT!

In 1939, there were 334,473 troops in the US military. By 1945, the number was 12,209,238.

Who Did Not Fight?

The only European countries that remained **neutral** during the war were Sweden, Ireland, and Switzerland, as well as Portugal and Spain and their colonies. Afghanistan, Turkey, and Yemen in the Middle East also remained neutral. Almost every other country in the world was involved in the war.

A squadron of US bombers patrol the coral reefs off Midway Island in the Pacific Ocean in 1942.

A World War?

War in Asia first broke out in 1931. By 1941, it had spread throughout Southeast Asia and into Oceania. War in Europe broke out in 1939 and spread throughout the Mediterranean and North Africa. Canada, and the rest of the Commonwealth and British Empire joined the fight against the **Axis** in 1939. They were followed by the United States in 1941. The other countries in the Americas, notably Brazil, had also joined the Allied cause by 1945.

The Battle of Stalingrad was one of the bloodiest battles in modern history and is considered a key turning point of WWII.

Adolf Hitler addresses Nazi supporters at a rally in 1933.

Causes of the War

Historians believe that World War I was one of the main causes of World War II. Germany lost the war and was heavily punished by the 1919 **Treaty of Versailles**, which took land away, restricted the size of its armed forces, and forced it to pay 132 billion gold marks in damages. Italy and Japan were on the winning side of the war but felt they had not received enough in reward. All three soon became extreme **dictatorships** and pledged to fight for a new world order, which they all hoped to dominate.

THE RISE OF HITLER

Adolf Hitler was born in Austria in 1889 and fought for Germany during World War I. In 1919, he joined a right-wing political group that would become the National Socialist German Workers Party (**Nazis**). Hitler adopted the swastika flag and in 1921 became the party's leader. By 1933, Hitler had enough support to be made Chancellor of Germany.

Adolf Hitler waving to crowds from his car.

"My Struggle"

In 1923, Hitler tried to seize power in Munich and was sent to prison. During his nine-month imprisonment he wrote a book about his political beliefs. *Mein Kampf* ("My Struggle") spelled out Hitler's hatred of both the Jews and **Communism**, and his desire to take land from Russia. Few people took the book seriously, but after he came to power, Hitler carried out most of his statements.

After the death of President Hindenburg in 1934, Adolf Hitler became the **"Führer"** (supreme leader) of Germany.

The Nazis in Power

Once in office, the Nazis took total control and crushed the opposition. Opponents were sent to concentration camps. Jews were stripped of all their rights and forbidden to marry non-Jews. Germany also illegally built up its armed forces.

8

Why Was Hitler Popular?

Many people supported Hitler because he told them what they wanted to hear. He promised to restore Germany to her former glory, to improve the quality of life and to ignore the Treaty of Versailles. He also used Jews, communists, capitalists, and other minority groups as scapegoats, blaming them for the country's problems.

Propaganda poster promoting the Nazi "fighting spirit."

The German American Bund

The German American Bund was formed in the US in 1937. Many of its members carried Nazi flags and dressed in uniforms with swastikas. In 1939, the Bund held a rally in New York City which attracted 20,000 people. After America entered the war, the Bund was outlawed.

Ancient Symbol

Hitler was not the first to use the swastika. Its use dates back thousands of years, to ancient civilizations in the Americas and Asia. The swastika originally symbolized good luck.

Nazi party members wore swastika armbands on their uniforms as a sign of their loyalty.

FASCIST ITALY

Italy had finished on the winning side of World War I but didn't feel that it had been awarded enough territory. The government was weak and divided. In 1922, Benito Mussolini, the leader of the National Fascist Party, came to power. Like Hitler, he set up a dictatorship and tried to crush any opposition to his rule.

Mussolini with his generals and Fascist troops as they march on Rome, October, 1922.

The Italian Empire

Unlike Britain or France, Italy did not have many **colonies** overseas, other than Somalia and Eritrea in East Africa. In 1911, Italy seized Libya in North Africa and some Turkish islands. Mussolini wanted to establish a new Roman **Empire** and dominate the Mediterranean Sea. In 1935–36, Italian forces overran Abyssinia (Ethiopia) in East Africa. Then in 1939, it seized Albania, opposite Italy in the Balkans.

Extent of the Italian Empire in 1939.

ITALY
ALBANIA
DODECANESE
LIBYA
ERITREA
ITALIAN SOMALILAND
ETHIOPIA

Italian Fascism

Fascists believed in **nationalism** and complete loyalty to their country. Above all, Fascists worshipped military strength. They aimed to unite their country into a disciplined force headed by a strong leader, or "Il Duce" ("the Leader"), as Mussolini was known. Like Hitler, Mussolini rallied support by promising his people glory. He used Italian sacrifices during World War I as one of his arguments for taking more territory. There were 670,000 Italians killed and over a million injured during the war. But Italy received "nothing but a few crumbs" at the peace table.

Front page of the *Daily Sketch* reporting the Italian invasion of Adowa, Abyssinia, in 1935.

HOW LONG WILL MUSSOLINI WANT? By CANDIDUS [WIRELESS: P. 23]

DAILY SKETCH FRIDAY, OCTOBER 4, 1935

DAILY SKETCH

ONE PENNY

SPECIAL WAR NUMBER

No. 8,249 (Registered as a newspaper)

FRIDAY, OCTOBER 4, 1935

DEVASTATION AT ADOWA

78 Bombs Dropped —1,700 Casualties | Big Battle Raging Late Last Night

What Happened During the Day

ADOWA — Planes drop 78 bombs—1700 casualties, including women and children—battle still raging this morning.

ADDIS ABABA — Preparing for attack expecting heavy air raids soon.

ADIGRAT — Bombed, women and children again among casualties, many houses damaged and destroyed.

WAL-WAL — Italians advancing northwards from here—historic spot where clash occurred last December.

A vivid impression of Adowa being bombed as visualised by artist from the latest reports.

FAST FACT!

In 1922, Italy became the first European country to turn fascist.

Black Shirts

All Italians were expected to obey Mussolini and his Fascist Party. Armed squads known as the Black Shirts helped to terrorize political opponents. One of their favorite punishments was to tie their victims to a tree and force them to drink castor oil or eat a live toad.

IMPERIAL JAPAN

During World War I, Japan fought with the Allies and quickly overran German colonies in China and the Pacific. But, like Germany, Japan was also hungry for more land. Japanese nationalists wanted to set up a Japanese empire in Asia and move away from American and Western influences.

FAST FACT!

The Rising Sun on the Imperial Japanese flag was meant to represent good fortune.

A Japanese anti-aircraft squad fires on Chinese planes in 1937.

War in China

Japan already controlled Korea and Taiwan. In 1931, Japanese forces seized Manchuria in northern China without the approval of the Japanese government. In 1937, war broke out between China and Japan. One year later, Japan announced a "New Order" or system of control in Asia dominated economically and militarily by Japan.

The Japanese State

In theory, Japan was a **democracy** controlled by parliament and ruled by the figurehead emperor, named Hirohito. But real power lay with the military and extreme nationalists outside parliament. In 1940, all of the political parties merged into the single Imperial Rule Assistance Association, setting up a one-party state.

Hirohito

Hirohito became emperor of Japan in 1926, reigning over the island nation for 62 years. As emperor, he did not have a direct say in what the government did, but he could make his influence felt. Historians cannot seem to agree whether the emperor supported or opposed Japan's policies of the 1930s.

Emperor Hirohito after his coronation in 1928.

The flag of the Imperial Japanese Navy.

A Growing Threat

In 1931, the Imperial Japanese Army numbered about 200,000 soldiers in 17 divisions. By 1941, the Imperial Japanese Army consisted of about 1,700,000 soldiers in 51 divisions.

The Nanking Massacre

In December 1937, after victory in the city of Shanghai, the Japanese attacked the Chinese capital of Nanking. After only four days of fighting, the battle was over and Nanking was in Japanese control. In the weeks that followed, Japanese troops killed around 300,000 civilians and soldiers, set fires and looted shops.

13

THE ROAD TO WAR

In 1936, Germany and Italy signed the Rome-Berlin Axis and became allies. Later that year, Germany and Japan signed the Anti-Comintern Pact against their mutual enemy, Soviet Russia. Italy joined this pact in 1937, creating the three-way alliance that would fight World War II together as the Axis powers.

The Opposition

Britain and France had fought Germany in World War I and were worried about German rearmament. The Soviet government distrusted Nazi Germany because of its hatred of communism. The USA, the most powerful nation in the world, did not want to get involved in fighting wars again and tried to stay out of international affairs.

Nazi flagbearers on parade at the Nuremberg party rally, 1933.

Rearmament

After 1933, Nazi Germany built up its armed services in defiance of the treaty that ended World War I. The Treaty of Versailles forbade Germany from having an army bigger than 100,000 men; but, in 1935, Hitler announced he intended to grow it to more than 500,000.

Conscription

To quickly build his army, Hitler introduced the military draft in 1935. It called for mandatory service for those between the ages of 18 and 45. During the war, the age range was extended to between 17 and 61. Most of those over the age of 35 would be reserves on standby.

Territorial Claims

In 1936, German troops reoccupied the German Rhineland. In 1938, Germany took control of Austria in the Anschluss (union). Both acts went against the Treaty of Versailles. Also in 1938, Germany occupied the German-speaking parts of Czechoslovakia. Britain and France had agreed that Germany could take that territory, so long as it promised not to seek any further territory in Europe. In March, 1939 Germany seized the rest of the country.

Hitler driving through the square of the old Imperial Palace, Vienna, during the Anschluss.

Rallying Support

Banners bearing the slogan "Those of the same blood belong in the same Reich!" were hung around Austria in early 1938 to rally support for its **annexation** into Germany. Though Hitler's troops had marched into Austria on March 12, a rigged nationwide vote was staged on April 10 to let the people decide for or against annexation. The vote came back 99% in favor.

FAST FACT!

The Treaty of Versailles was a lengthy document, containing 440 Articles.

15

1939: THE YEAR WAR BEGAN

In 1939, Hitler decided on a war of conquest against its eastern European neighbor, Poland. Britain and France promised to support Poland if Germany invaded. On September 1, 1939, Germany invaded Poland. France and Britain both declared war on Germany on September 3rd. A few weeks later Russia invaded Poland from the east.

FAST FACT!

In 1939, Europe went to war for the second time in 25 years.

ATLANTIC OCEAN

PORTUGAL

German machine gunner during the first days of the war, September 16, 1939.

German plane flying over Poland, 1939.

Key Events

AUGUST 23
Germany signs secret Nazi-Soviet **Pact** with **USSR** (see page 18).

SEPTEMBER 1
Germany invades Poland (see page 20).

SEPTEMBER 3
Britain and France declare war on Germany (see page 20).

NORWAY · SWEDEN · FINLAND

DENMARK

North Sea

Baltic Sea

Estonia

Latvia

Lithuania

East Prussia

UNITED KINGDOM

London ★

NETHER-LANDS

BELGIUM

Berlin ★

GERMANY

Poland

USSR

Paris ★

FRANCE

SWITZ-ERLAND

SLOVAKIA

HUNGARY

ROMANIA

Black Sea

PAIN

Corsica

Rome ★

ITALY

YUGOSLAVIA

BULGARIA

Sardinia

Albania

TURKEY

GREECE

Syria (France)

Dodecanese (Italy)

Cyprus (Britain)

Sicily (Italy)

Lebanon (France)

Malta (Britain)

Mediterranean Sea

Palestine (Britain)

Tunisia (France)

Libya (Italy)

EGYPT (British Protectorate)

KEY

Axis Powers (end of 1939)

Allies (end of 1939)

Neutral Nations

Molotov-Ribbentrop Pact Line

0   300 miles
0   300 kilometers

SEPTEMBER 4
Japan declares neutrality.

SEPTEMBER 5
United States declares neutrality.

SEPTEMBER 10
Canada declares war on Germany.

SEPTEMBER 17
USSR occupies eastern Poland.

OCTOBER 16
Germans attack the British at Firth of Forth.

17

THE NAZI-SOVIET PACT

In one of the great turnarounds in modern history, two fierce opponents suddenly agreed with each other. Germany's intention was eventually to crush Soviet Russia. First, it had to invade Poland. Russia was scared by Germany's power, so in April 1939, they proposed an alliance with Britain and France against Germany. These two nations were slow to respond, so in August 1939, Russia signed a surprise non-aggression pact with Nazi Germany. Both countries agreed to remain neutral if the other was at war.

The Treaty of Nonaggression

ARTICLE I said that Germany and the Soviet Union would "desist from any act of violence, any aggressive action, and any attack on each other, either individually or jointly with other powers."

ARTICLE II said that if one country was under attack "by a third power" the other would not assist the third country.

ARTICLE III said that the two governments should "maintain continual contact with one another . . . to exchange information on problems affecting their common interests."

ARTICLE IV said that neither country should "participate in any grouping of powers whatsoever that is directly or indirectly aimed at the other party."

ARTICLE V said that if disputes arose between Germany and the Soviet Union, "both parties shall settle these disputes or conflicts exclusively through friendly exchange of opinion."

ARTICLE VI said that the treaty was good for ten years with an option to extend it for five more years.

What Germany Gained

Germany and Russia agreed to divide Poland between them. When Germany invaded Poland on September 1, 1939, it knew Russia would not interfere. Above all, the pact gave Germany more time to prepare to fight Russia.

Cartoon showing the unexpected alliance between Hitler and Stalin.

The treaty is also known as the Molotov-Ribbentrop Pact after the Soviet and Nazi ministers who signed the agreement in 1939.

FAST FACT!
The Nazi-Soviet Pact was signed in Moscow.

What Russia Gained

Stalin knew that Hitler could not be trusted, but the pact bought him time to re-arm for when Hitler did invade Russia. Germany also agreed to let Russia invade eastern Poland, Estonia, Latvia and Lithuania. On March 13, 1941, Russia signed a peace treaty with Japan. Germany and Japan could now act without fear of a Russian response.

19

THE INVASION OF POLAND

Germany demanded the German-speaking port of Danzig and the strip of Polish land that separated Germany from its East Prussian province. When Poland refused, Germany prepared to invade. The attack began on September 1 and was soon successful. After Russia invaded eastern Poland on September 17, the country temporarily ceased to exist.

A Jewish man walking past bomb damaged buildings in Poland during the early days of the war.

German soldiers invading Poland, at the beginning of World War II.

FAST FACT!

2,750 German tanks and 2,315 aircraft attacked Poland's 880 tanks and 400 aircraft.

Blitzkrieg

More than 1,500,000 Germans attacked Poland using a technique that became known as **Blitzkrieg** ("Lightning War"). This attack consisted of a large number of tanks and armored vehicles supported by a heavy air bombardment that quickly overwhelmed the Polish army.

The War Begins

Britain and France had agreed to support Poland if it was attacked. So when Germany invaded Poland, Britain and France declared war on Germany. The two countries and their vast overseas empires became known as the **Allies** because they were allied against the Germans. In a letter to Mussolini on August 25, Hitler made it seem like Poland was a threat to Germany. He also said that the Polish had fired on German aircraft.

"We have been for weeks in a state of alarm as a result of the Polish mobilization . . . last night alone there were twenty-one Polish border violations . . . there is a limit beyond which I will not be pushed under any circumstances."

—Adolf Hitler to Mussolini, August 25, 1939

Hitler making a speech after the German invasion of Poland.

Casualties

It is estimated that between 8,000 to 20,000 Germans were killed and 30,000 injured in the invasion. The Polish suffered 66,000 dead and 134,000 injured, with nearly 700,000 prisoners of war taken. The Soviets lost over 1,000 men with about 2,000 injured.

THE PHONY WAR

After Germany and Russia had swallowed up Poland between them, Europe enjoyed a period of relative peace known as the Phony War. Both sides used the time to strengthen their armed forces and prepare for more war.

The Winter War

The only fighting that took place broke out between Russia and Finland in November 1939. Russia attacked Finland to gain more territory to protect its northern city of Leningrad. The Finns bravely fought back in the snow but were eventually overwhelmed and forced to make peace in March 1940.

A group of Finnish alpine troops or "ghost troops" on skis.

Britain and France Get Ready

Everyone in Britain was given a gas mask to protect them against possible German gas attacks. Bomb shelters were built in public parks to shelter people from explosions. A blackout was imposed—street and car lights had to be turned off after dark. People covered their doors and windows with thick curtains to prevent any light from showing. Ration books were introduced to limit certain foods so that everyone had enough to eat. The French, meanwhile, built up their armed forces.

The Firth of Forth

On October 16, 1939, the Germans attacked Britain by air for the first time. Nine German planes bombed the Royal Navy at Rosyth, near the Firth of Forth in Scotland. The British were taken by surprise. 16 Royal Navy personnel were killed and 44 wounded in the attack. British airplanes scrambled to counter-attack and downed two German planes.

Another Treaty

The German-Soviet Boundary and Friendship Treaty of September 28, 1939, officially proclaimed the boundary between the German-controlled part of former Poland and the Soviet portion. It also proclaimed that the treaty signified "a firm foundation for a progressive development of the friendly relations between their peoples."

British citizens, some waving the cardboard cases holding their gas masks, head into a London shelter during the first air raid warning on the day Britain declared war.

British No. 111 Squadron Hawker Hurricanes during the hard winter of 1939-40.

1940: EUROPE FALLS

By mid 1940, much of Europe was controlled by the Axis powers (Germany and Italy). With the fall of France and the evacuation at Dunkirk, the Allies had been kicked out of Europe, and Britain was now alone in the fight against the Axis. As the months passed, the world waited nervously to see what would happen next.

Maginot Line, on the French German border. British troops march over bridge into the French underground fortress. Fall 1940.

FAST FACT!

Bombing was unofficially postponed by both sides between December 24–27, 1940.

IRELAND
UNITED KINGDOM

London ★

BELGIUM

Paris ★
FRANCE

VICHY FRANCE

ANDORRA

PORTUGAL

SPAIN

●**Gibraltar**
(Britain)
SPANISH MOROCCO

ATLANTIC OCEAN

Morocco
(Vichy France)

Algeria
(Vichy France)

Spanish Sahara

Key Events

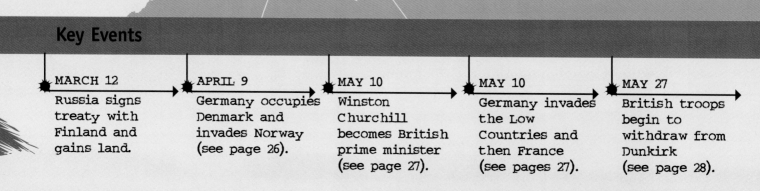

MARCH 12	APRIL 9	MAY 10	MAY 10	MAY 27
Russia signs treaty with Finland and gains land.	Germany occupies Denmark and invades Norway (see page 26).	Winston Churchill becomes British prime minister (see page 27).	Germany invades the Low Countries and then France (see pages 27).	British troops begin to withdraw from Dunkirk (see page 28).

KEY

■	*Axis Powers and Axis occupied (end of 1940)*
■	*Allies (end of 1940)*
■	*Neutral Nations*
★	*Capital city*

0   300 miles

0   300 kilometers

NORWAY

SWEDEN

FINLAND

DENMARK

NETH.

North Sea

Estonia

Latvia

Baltic Sea

Lithuania

Moscow ★

Berlin ★

GERMANY

East Prussia

USSR

White Russia

POLAND

Ukraine

SWITZ.

SLOVAKIA

HUNGARY

ROMANIA

Crimea

Adriatic Sea

YUGOSLAVIA

Black Sea

Corsica

Rome ★

ITALY

BULGARIA

Sardinia

Albania

GREECE

TURKEY

IRAN

Sicily

Malta
(Britain)

Dodecanese
(Italy)

Cyprus
(Britain)

Syria
(Vichy France)

IRAQ

Tunisia
(Vichy France)

Lebanon
(Vichy France)

Mediterranean Sea

Palestine
(Britain)

Transjordan
(Britain)

SAUDI ARABIA

Tripolitania

Cyrenaica

EGYPT
(Britain)

LIBYA

JUNE 10
Italy enters war on German side and invades France.

JUNE 22
France signs peace agreement with Germany.

JULY 10
Battle of Britain begins in the skies above England (see page 34).

SEPTEMBER 7
Germany begins Blitz against British cities (see page 36).

SEPTEMBER 12
Italy attacks British-run Egypt, and later, Greece.

25

THE GERMANS ATTACK

The German attacks against Scandinavia and the Low Countries were quick and effective. Soon these countries were part of the German **Third Reich** (the Nazi empire). The invasion of France took longer. The Germans were helped by the Italians who joined the war and attacked southern France in early June.

German infantrymen fighting for control of Norway in the snow.

Scandinavia

The Allies wanted to prevent Germany from importing much-needed Swedish iron ore through Norwegian ports. The Germans wanted to control Norway to use it as a base against attacks on British shipping in the North Atlantic. In April, German troops poured into Denmark and then Norway, rapidly gaining control of both countries.

The Low Countries

The easiest route for the German armies to attack France lay through the Netherlands, Belgium, and Luxembourg, also known as the "Low" countries. On May 10, German troops attacked. The three countries were too small and weak to defend themselves and surrendered. Their governments fled into exile in London.

Rotterdam

On May 14, 1940 German bombers attacked the city of Rotterdam.

On May 14, the Germans began a devastating attack on the Dutch city of Rotterdam. A ten-minute air raid resulted in a huge firestorm that destroyed the historic center of the city and killed around 900 residents. A total of 2,200 Dutch soldiers died trying to defend their country against the Nazis.

Leopold Wouldn't Leave

Belgian King Leopold III surrendered to the Germans and chose to remain in Belgium rather than flee and form a government in exile. Some claimed he was being a traitor by doing so, but he believed he was being patriotic by not abandoning his countrymen.

Churchill for PM

Winston Churchill

Neville Chamberlain was prime minister of Britain at the start of the war but, in May 1940, lost the confidence of Parliament. His successor was Winston Churchill, a leading politician for many years. Churchill set up a multi-party government and soon inspired the British people with his reassuring and rousing speeches.

EVACUATION AT DUNKIRK

Hundreds of thousands of British troops, part of the BEF (British Expeditionary Force) were in France in the spring of 1940, helping the French protect their country against German invasion. After the Germans began to make headway into France, Allied troops were soon trapped near the coast of northern France. Prime Minister Churchill ordered that the British forces be evacuated rather than risk capture.

British soldiers wade out to a rescue ship waiting off the beach at Dunkirk.

FAST FACT!

68,111 British troops were killed, injured or captured in France between May and early June.

The Great Escape

Although Dunkirk was technically a military defeat, the evacuation efforts (codenamed Operation Dynamo) saved a total of 338,226 troops between May 27 and June 4, about 140,000 of which were French troops. The Royal Air Force was instrumental in helping protect the transports and keep the Germans at bay. On May 27 alone, 16 squadrons of RAF fighters flew over Dunkirk.

Thousands of soldiers line up to be evacuated from Dunkirk.

Little Ships

The evacuation was conducted mainly by Royal Navy destroyers, backed up by all kinds of other boats—including ferries, fishing boats, and pleasure boats. Almost a third of the 933 ships involved in the evacuation were either sunk or damaged by the Germans. Among the civilian boats that helped evacuate were: Aquabelle, a 45-foot yacht; Miss Margate, a 26-foot motor cruiser, which, at 43 mph was the fastest civilian boat at Dunkirk; Ferry Nymph, a 41-foot ferry that could carry up to 90 troops; Windsong, a 44-foot sailboat; and Viking, an 87-foot barge.

British stamp commemorating the soldiers of Dunkirk.

Not Everyone Made It

The British Destroyer HMS *Wakeful* was the greatest casualty of Operation Dynamo. This ship, carrying more than 600 troops toward England, was torpedoed on May 29. The torpedo hit the ammunition magazine and was sunk in just 15 seconds, with the loss of nearly everyone on board.

Left Behind

The first priority was evacuating soldiers. A great deal of equipment had to be left behind:
- 2,472 guns
- 63,879 vehicles
- 20,548 motorcycles
- 76,097 tons of ammunition
- 416,940 tons of stores

THE FALL OF FRANCE

On May 10, 1940, German troops invaded northern France. A month later, Italy joined the war on the Axis side and invaded southern France. About 360,000 French soldiers were killed or wounded. The end came quickly. Paris was occupied on June 14, and an armistice between the two sides signed on June 22. France was now under German control and split in two. Britain, under Winston Churchill, fought on alone.

German troops celebrate the Fall of France with a victory parade in Paris.

Adolf Hitler in front of the Eiffel Tower in Paris. The city was occupied by German troops on June 14, 1940.

The Eiffel Tower

On June 23, 1940—just after the fall of France—Hitler flew to Paris for a sightseeing tour of the city, during which this photo was taken of him standing in front of the Eiffel Tower. In August 1944, Hitler ordered that the historic tower be demolished, but the order was never carried out.

Vichy France

After the German invasion of France, the French prime minister, Marshal Philippe Pétain, a hero of World War I, made peace with Germany. The Germans occupied the north and west of France while Pétain headed a government for the south and east based at the small town of Vichy. The Vichy government collaborated and cooperated with the Germans but was later reduced to a puppet regime after the Allies invaded French North Africa in November 1942.

The Armistice agreement between Germany and France was signed on a train car at Rethondes station near Compiègne.

FAST FACT!

The French town Le Chambon-Sur-Lignon sheltered between 1,000–5,000 Jews during the war.

FRENCH RESISTANCE

Resistance to the occupation of France began immediately, both within France, and in countries such as England. In 1940, a group called the **Free French** was organized to rally worldwide support for the cause of fighting the Nazis in general, and also against the Nazi occupation of France.

Parade of Free French in London, 1940.

Charles de Gaulle appealed to the French to resist German rule.

A Rallying Cry

Charles de Gaulle was a French army commander who refused to accept the armistice with Germany. He fled to London, where on June 18, 1940 he broadcast an appeal on the radio to the French to resist German rule. It was the official beginning of the French Resistance: "Believe me, I speak to you with full knowledge of the facts and tell you that nothing is lost for France. The same means that overcame us can bring us to a day of victory. For France is not alone! She is not alone! . . . Whatever happens, the flame of the French resistance must not be extinguished and will not be extinguished. Tomorrow, as today, I will speak on Radio London."

Spreading the Word

In July 1940, an "Appeal to all French People" poster was put up around England. It was signed by De Gaulle, and contained a shortened version of his speech of June 18, in both French and English, including the words "France has lost a battle, but France has not lost the war."

Moulin's Mission

Jean Moulin, a former government official who'd escaped from France to England in late 1941, was sent back to France by Charles De Gaulle a few months later with the mission of coordinating the French Resistance movement with the Free French. He spent more than a year organizing before he was captured in 1943. He was tortured, and eventually died on a train bound for Germany.

Jean Moulin.

33

THE BATTLE OF BRITAIN

After the fall of France, Hitler turned his attention to Operation Sealion, the invasion of Britain. First, he had to gain supremacy of the skies from the British Royal Air Force (RAF). On July 10, 1940, the Luftwaffe (German Air Force) began attacking shipping in the English Channel. In August, waves of German bombers attacked ports and airfields, while German fighter pilots battled with British, Czech, Polish, Canadian, and Australian pilots in the skies.

Pilots of No. 303 (Polish) Squadron, the most successful Fighter Command unit during the Battle of Britain.

The Air Threat

Britain had been wary of German air power since World War I, when German bombs killed more than 1,000 British people. As the years passed and technology improved, fear of an attack by Germany grew, especially after Hitler formed the Luftwaffe in February 1935. The Luftwaffe began with 1,888 planes and grew from there.

Pilot Shortage

The British were in desperate need of pilots, so they accepted men from British territories and other countries into the Royal Air Force. Nearly 20% of the 3,000 pilots who fought in the Battle of Britain were from countries other than England. The top pilot of the Battle of Britain was Sergeant Josef František, from Czechoslovakia, who downed 17 German planes.

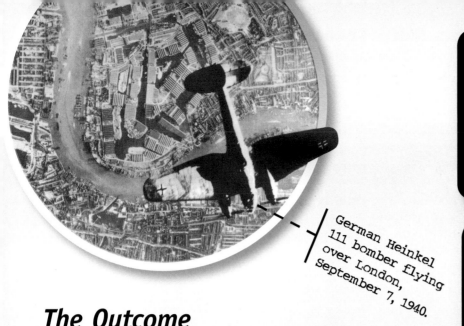

German Heinkel 111 bomber flying over London, September 7, 1940.

British and Allied Losses

- 1,547 aircraft destroyed
- 544 aircrew killed
- 422 aircrew wounded

German Losses

- 1,887 aircraft destroyed
- 2,698 aircrew killed
- 967 aircrew captured

The Outcome

On September 15, now known as "Battle of Britain Day," the Luftwaffe launched a massive assault that they believed would lead to a successful invasion. The RAF fought off the attack and on September 17, Hitler suspended Operation Sealion indefinitely.

The Main German Attacks

- July 10–August 11: British shipping in the English Channel and the main Channel ports, such as Portsmouth
- August 12–23: Coastal airfields
- August 24–September 6: Main military airfields
- September 7 onward: British towns and cities

THE BLITZ

On September 7, 1940, German bombers attacked London. They returned on 57 consecutive nights, while bombers also attacked 15 other major British cities. The Blitz, as the British called this campaign, killed around 40,000 people and wounded many more. More than one million buildings were damaged before the Germans stopped on May 21, 1941.

St. Paul's Cathedral in London became a symbol of hope for the British during the Blitz. It was hit and set ablaze, but luckily it remained intact.

Blitz Spirit

The Germans tried to bomb the British into surrender. Their aim was to form a blockade by attacking supplies and ports, and destroying factories. But war industries continued to operate and the bombing had little effect on morale; people did not lose hope.

FAST FACT!

During the Blitz, the Germans dropped 18,800 tons of bombs on London.

Children at War

When war broke out in 1939, many British children were evacuated out of London to live in the country, safe from the bombs. Parents tried to protect their children from the worst effects of the war, but their education was disrupted and sometimes their homes were destroyed. Worst of all, some children had to cope with the death of family members in the war.

Children from Chelsea in London get ready for evacuation.

Ruins of Coventry Cathedral after heavy bombing by the Germans.

Coventry

One of the worst attacks took place in the city of Coventry on November 14, 1940. Coventry had many munitions factories and was a prime German target. More than 500 German bombers attacked the city, dropping high explosive and **incendiary bombs.** The city center was completely destroyed, including the famous old cathedral.

Churchill's Speech

British Prime Minister Winston Churchill knew the Germans were going to attack. On June 18, 1940, he gave a speech preparing his nation for the worst: "Let us therefore brace ourselves to our duties and so bear ourselves that, if the British Empire and its Commonwealth last for a thousand years, men will still say: This was their finest hour."

SPIES AND SPYING

During the war, both sides used spies to find out what their enemies were up to. The spies passed information about troop movements, government plans, and other important facts. Codebreakers tried to crack enemy codes, while special operations soldiers launched daring raids into enemy territory to blow up important targets such as railroad yards and power stations.

A German Enigma machine. British codebreakers were eventually able to decode Enigma messages.

Bletchley Park

German military messages were coded using the fiendishly complex Enigma machine. While at Bletchley Park in England, mathematician Alan Turing invented an electromechanical device known as the Bombe which enabled codebreakers to decode the Enigma's messages. Colossus, the world's first programmable computer, was also built at Bletchley. The work of the codebreakers was essential in defeating enemy **U-boats** in the North Atlantic and helping the Allies at D-Day. Their top-secret work was only made public in the 1970s.

Bletchley Park, the headquarters of Britain's top secret codebreakers.

The SOE

In July 1940, the British government set up the Special Operations Executive (SOE) to conduct spying, sabotage, and fact-finding in occupied Europe and to help local resistance groups. Among its most famous acts was the kidnapping of the top German general Heinrich Kreipe in Crete in April 1944.

FAST FACT!

The British spy nicknamed "White Rabbit" inspired many James Bond stories.

A member of the Women's Royal Naval Service at Bletchley with Colossus, the world's first electronic programmable computer.

Super Spies

Spies were armed with some extraordinary gadgets and weapons in their secret war against the enemy. Ordinary everyday objects such as pipes, handkerchiefs, or playing cards were transformed into clever devices that allowed spies to smuggle escape aids to prisoners of war, to store information, or to listen-in on the enemy. Other tools of the trade included plaster cow manure or camel dung packed with plastic explosives, exploding rats, and itching powder.

1941: THE WAR GOES GLOBAL

In June, Germany invaded Soviet Russia, starting a titanic battle in eastern Europe. In December, Japan unexpectedly attacked the US fleet at Pearl Harbor in Hawaii, bringing both countries into the war. Every continent and ocean was now at war. The fighting was brutal and bloodthirsty.

ARCTIC OCEAN

NORWAY
SWEDEN
FINLAND
Baltic Sea
North Sea
IRELAND
UNITED KINGDOM
GERMANY
POLAND
BELGIUM
FRANCE
HUNGARY
VICHY FRANCE
CROATIA
ROM.
BULG.
Black Sea
ITALY
PORTUGAL
SPAIN
GREECE
TURKEY
Mediterranean Sea
IRAQ
IRAN
MOROCCO (V. Fr.)
TUNISIA (V. Fr.)
ALGERIA (Vichy France)
LIBYA (Italy)
EGYPT
SAUDI ARABIA
SPANISH SAHARA
Red Sea
ERITREA
ADEN
FRENCH WEST AFRICA (Vichy France)
ANGLO-EGYPTIAN SUDAN
GOLD COAST (Britain)
NIGERIA (Britain)
CAMEROON
FRENCH EQUATORIAL AFRICA
ETHIOPIA
ITALIAN EAST AFRICA
SIERRA LEONE (Britain)
LIBERIA
KENYA (Britain)
UGANDA (Britain)
BELGIAN CONGO
TANGANYIKA (Britain)
SOUTH ATLANTIC OCEAN
ANGOLA (Port.)
N. RHODESIA
S. RHODESIA
MOZAMBIQUE (Portugal)
MADAGASCAR (Vichy France)
SOUTH WEST AFRICA
BECHUANA LAND
SOUTH AFRICA

The Battle of Moscow was Germany's first major retreat of the war.

Key Events

MARCH 4
British troops land in Greece to help expel Italian forces.

APRIL 6
Germany invades Yugoslavia and Greece (see page 43).

MAY 16
Italian troops surrender to the British in East Africa.

JUNE 1
British troops leave Crete, their last foothold in Europe.

JUNE 22
Germany attacks USSR in Operation Barbarossa (see page 44).

KEY

AXIS AND AXIS-HELD
(end of 1941)

ALLIES AND ALLIED-HELD
(end of 1941)

NEUTRAL NATIONS

→ Main lines of Axis advance

— Axis front line

1 Battle of the Atlantic
2 Leningrad
3 Pearl Harbor
4 Bataan
5 Malaya

SOVIET UNION

ALASKA
(USA)

AFGHANISTAN

MONGOLIA

MANCHUKO
(Japan)

CHINA

KOREA
(Japan)

JAPAN

PACIFIC
OCEAN

3

HAWAIIAN
ISLANDS
(USA)

INDIA
(Britain)

BURMA
(Britain)

Bay of
Bengal

SIAM FRENCH
INDO-
CHINA

4

PHILIPPINES

GUAM
(USA)

MARSHALL
ISLANDS
(Japan)

Arabian
Sea

CEYLON
(Britain)

BRITISH
MALAYA

5

CAROLINE ISLANDS
(Japan)

INDIAN

OCEAN

DUTCH EAST INDIES

NORTHEAST
NEW GUINEA

SOLOMON
ISLANDS
(Britain)

PAPUA
(Australia)

SAMOA

NEW
HEBRIDES
(France/Britain)

FIJI
(Britain)

NEW
CALEDONIA
(France)

AUSTRALIA

FAST FACT!

Two major world powers, the USA and USSR, now became allies in the war.

NEW ZEALAND

JULY 28
Japanese occupy
French Indo-China.

SEPTEMBER 15
German troops
begin 872-day siege
of Leningrad (see
page 46).

NOVEMBER 23
Germans get
within 35 miles
of Moscow

DECEMBER 7
Japan bombs US
fleet at Pearl
Harbor (see
page 52).

DECEMBER 8
Japanese attack
the Philippines
and then
Malaya (see
page 54).

INVADING THE BALKANS

German army units invading Greece in April 1941

The Germans needed to secure the Balkans before they could attack Russia. In October 1940, Italy attacked Greece but was soon halted. After attacking Yugoslavia in April 1941, German forces invaded Greece to help their Italian allies. The British tried but failed to support the Greeks. Germany gained the support of Romania, whose oil it desperately needed for the forthcoming attack on Russia, and other countries in the Balkans.

Greek soldiers in Albania, fighting the Italian invasion of Greece.

The Tripartite Pact

On September 27, 1940, Germany, Italy, and Japan signed the Tripartite Pact to fight together. Hungary, Romania, and Bulgaria joined by the end of the year.

On March 25, 1941, Yugoslavia joined but withdrew two days later when its government was overthrown. Germany therefore invaded the country and divided it up with Italy.

42

Invading Greece

Greek troops were concentrated on their northwest border with Albania fighting the Italians. On April 6, German troops attacked from Bulgaria moving around behind the Greek troops. The Greeks were outnumbered and out-maneuvered. By April 30, they had surrendered.

A Country No More

After invading Yugoslavia, the Axis powers carved up the country. Germany took parts of Slovenia and set up a government in Serbia. Italy took parts of Slovenia, as well as areas along the Adriatic coast. Other pieces of the former country went to Hungary, Bulgaria, and Albania.

German troops crossing the Pineiós river during the invasion of Greece.

FAST FACT!

The Germans raised the swastika flag over the Acropolis in Athens as a sign of victory.

Italy's Failed Attempt

In October 1940, Italian troops invaded Greece from Albania (which had been annexed by Italy), but it was only a matter of days before the Greeks pushed back and sent the Italians back into Albania.

Resisting Occupation

The occupation of Yugoslavia was not without difficulties. Following the invasion, there was a strong armed resistance by various Communist groups backed by the Soviet Union. In 1941, the Germans had to take several actions to try to suppress these fighters.

OPERATION BARBAROSSA

On June 22, 1941, three vast Axis army groups poured over the Russian border. The Russians were caught by surprise and quickly lost their entire air force and 600,000 men. This was the fight that would help to decide the future of the war.

German troops with an anti-tank gun during the advance into Russia.

Who Was Barbarossa?

Frederick Barbarossa ruled Germany as Holy Roman Emperor from 1155 to 1190. His name meant "red beard" in Italian. Barbarossa was famous for his bravery and skill, which was why his name was chosen for this campaign.

Early Planning

Hitler issued Directive No. 21 on December 18, 1940, which said "The German armed forces must be ready, even before the war against England is over, to crush Soviet Russia with a rapid field campaign." He was especially concerned that the German Air Force be ready both to support the army and protect Germany from attack by air, helping bring the invasion to a "speedy conclusion."

Barbarossa in Numbers

- 3.8 million Axis soldiers invaded the USSR
- 4,300 Axis tanks
- 4,389 Axis aircraft
- 7,200 Axis artillery pieces
- 1,800 miles length of the front line
- 5.5 million Russian soldiers defended their homeland
- 25,000 Russian tanks
- 11,357 Russian aircraft
- 800,000 Axis casualties
- 5 million Russian casualties

A Little Help from their Friends

The Germans attacked using not only their own forces, but also those of their allies. The initial attack against the Soviets included 650,000 troops from Finland and Romania. Later, the Russian campaign was supplemented by troops from Italy, Hungary, Slovakia, and Croatia.

Tank Elimination

Bombing of strategic targets was critical to success in Russia. German Stuka airplanes used their 37 mm cannons to fire at sitting duck Russian tanks. One of the most successful pilots in the history of air warfare was Hans-Ulrich Rudel, who was part of the invasion force and destroyed more than 500 enemy tanks and 1,000 other vehicles in his career.

FAST FACT!

Operation Barbarossa was the largest invasion in the history of warfare.

KEY

- **AXIS POWERS AND AXIS-OCCUPIED** (end of 1941)
- **ALLIES** (end of 1941)
- **NEUTRAL NATIONS**
- **LINES OF ADVANCE OF GERMAN PANZER GROUPS**
- **Front line 30 September 1941**
- **Line of furthest German advance in 1941**

0 — 300 miles
0 — 300 kilometers

FINLAND
Helsinki★
Leningrad
Estonia
Latvia
●Riga
Lithuania
●Memel
●Danzig
East Prussia
Minsk●
White Russia
★Warsaw
POLAND
Smolensk●
★Moscow
USSR
●Kiev
Ukraine
Budapest
★ HUNGARY
CROATIA
ROMANIA
●Odessa
Crimea
Sevastapol●
Black Sea
Rostov

THE SIEGE OF LENINGRAD

On September 8, 1941, the German Army Group North began to besiege the northern Russian city of Leningrad. Hitler was determined to starve the city into surrender. German guns pounded the city for 872 days until the siege was finally broken on January 27, 1944.

Trucks carrying supplies across Lake Lagoda to Leningrad.

The Ice Road

During the winter, Lake Ladoga froze over and trucks were able to take food and other supplies into Leningrad. When the trucks left they took refugees with them.

Why Leningrad?

Leningrad was one of Russia's oldest, largest, and most important cities. Capturing Leningrad was a key part of the overall invasion of the Soviet Union. However, an all-out battle would take too much manpower. Hitler hoped that a blockade would force the city to surrender quickly.

The Leningrad Symphony

Russian composer Dmitri Shostakovich worked as a firefighter in Leningrad. His Symphony No. 7—the Leningrad Symphony—was performed by the Radio Orchestra in the city during the siege and broadcast to the German lines through loudspeakers. The performance boosted morale in the city and disheartened the Germans.

Dmitri Shostakovich

- 642,000 civilians killed during the siege
- 1,107,881 Russian troops killed or wounded
- 610,000 German soldiers killed or wounded

A Deadly Winter

The winter of 1941/42 was a cold and deadly one for the citizens of Leningrad. Electricity was almost nonexistent and fuel for heating homes was scarce. Bombs and cold weather destroyed water pipes, and people had to get water from holes in the ice in the Neva River.

Evacuating Leningrad

During the summer of 1941, the Soviets began to evacuate Leningrad. On June 29, the first trains carrying about 15,000 children left the city, but some of them headed straight toward the advancing Germans, who attacked the rail lines and forced the trains to return to Leningrad. By August 29, a total of 636,000 people of all ages had been evacuated.

FAST FACT!

People were so hungry during the siege that they ate dogs, cats, horses, and rats.

TOBRUK AND NORTH AFRICA

In September 1940, Italian troops invaded British-occupied Egypt in an attempt to seize the Suez Canal. The British quickly pushed the Italian armies back into next-door Libya. In February 1941, Hitler sent one of his top generals—Erwin Rommel —to help the Italians. Fighting between the Axis and Allied armies concentrated on the port of Tobruk.

German General Rommel with the 15th Panzer Division in North Africa, 1941.

FAST FACT!

Soldiers fighting in the Egyptian deserts had to check their boots for scorpions every morning.

The Siege

On April 10, 1941, Rommel attacked the city of Tobruk, which was being held by British Commonwealth troops. On November 27, the Allied 8th Army finally broke the siege.

Victory Then Defeat

The Allied victory at Tobruk was not a permanent one. In May 1942, Rommel attacked again, capturing Tobruk on June 21. It was a bitter blow to the Allies—British Egypt was now in danger.

British soldiers at war in the deserts of North Africa.

Why Tobruk?

The Allies needed Tobruk and its harbor to defend Egypt and the Suez Canal. Without Tobruk, the Axis had to bring their supplies overland from Tripoli, 930 miles away. Both sides wanted the town.

A British anti-aircraft gun crew in Tobruk.

The Desert Fox

General Rommel was so aggressive and smart while leading the German army through North Africa that he earned the nickname "The Desert Fox". He was highly respected by Allied leaders.

Dive Bombers

In April 1941, a total of 386 German Air Force dive-bomber planes took part in 21 dive bombing attacks at Tobruk. These raids were designed to hit strategic targets and strike fear in the Allies. The Allies were desperate to stop the German bombers from succeeding. Allied anti-aircraft guns at Tobruk fired 34,111 rounds of ammunition against German planes in April 1941 alone.

THE BATTLE OF THE ATLANTIC

Every week, Britain imported around one million tons of much-needed supplies in convoys of ships sailing across the Atlantic. Without these supplies its people would starve and its armies would run out of weapons. In a campaign that lasted the length of the war, German surface ships and U-boats (submarines) attacked the convoys, sinking many ships.

The Battle

At first, the German U-boats had the upper hand. More than 270 Allied ships were sunk from June to October 1940 alone. Then the Allies developed better anti-submarine weapons and overcame German surface ships by the end of 1942. By 1943, the German U-boats had been mostly defeated, although attacks continued until the end of the war.

Coastguardsmen on the deck of the US coastguard cutter Spencer watch the destruction of a Nazi U-boat.

FAST FACT!

The Battle of the Atlantic was the longest military campaign of the war.

The Battle in Numbers

- 100 Allied convoys attacked
- 1,000 individual Allied ships attacked
- 36,200 Allied sailors killed
- 36,000 Allied merchant seamen killed
- 3,500 Allied merchant ships sunk
- 175 Allied warships sunk
- 30,000 Axis sailors killed
- 783 Axis submarines sunk

In Convoy

Individual ships were very vulnerable to attack. Therefore the Allies organized **convoys** of between 30 and 70 merchant ships which were protected by heavily armed warships. Later in the war, improved radar and new aircraft helped defend the convoys better.

A convoy crossing the ocean during the Battle of the Atlantic.

U-Boats

A typical German Unterseeboot or U-boat was 250 feet long, weighed 1,260 tons, and could travel at 19 knots on the surface and 7.3 knots submerged. U-boats were equipped with torpedoes to use when under the surface and deck guns while on the surface. The Allies tracked them with sonar detection and airborne radar equipment.

PEARL HARBOR

As Japanese and American diplomats discussed a peace settlement to end their war in China, a Japanese fleet steamed toward the US naval base of Pearl Harbor in Hawaii. On the morning of December 7, 1941, Japanese naval aircraft attacked Pearl Harbor. The Americans were caught totally by surprise. The US was now at war with Japan and its Axis allies.

FAST FACT!

After Pearl Harbor, Roosevelt used Al Capone's bulletproof car to protect him from assassins.

Pearl Harbor shortly after the attack. One day later, the US declared war on Japan.

Why Did Japan Attack?

During 1941, Japan continued to invade China and occupied French Indo-China. In response, Britain, France, and the Dutch East Indies stopped all trade with Japan. Japan retaliated by attacking the US. They wanted to prevent the American fleet from interfering when Japan invaded the rest of Southeast Asia to secure its oil and other supplies.

The *Arizona*

The 34,000-ton, 600-foot-long battleship USS *Arizona* was one of the targets hit by the Japanese on December 7, 1941. The 27-year-old ship sustained eight bomb hits, including one that penetrated the deck and set off a tremendous explosion and fire. A total of 1,177 of the 1,400 crewmen were killed. A memorial to the sunken ship was built in 1961.

Destruction of the USS Arizona, December 7, 1941.

Japan

- 5 midget submarines sunk or grounded
- 29 aircraft destroyed
- 64 men killed

United States

- 4 battleships sunk
- 2 battleships sunk (but later recovered)
- 13 ships damaged
- 188 aircraft destroyed
- 159 aircraft damaged
- 2,403 men killed
- 1,178 men wounded

She Voted No

When Congress voted on a war resolution against Japan, the tally in the House of Representatives was 388-1. The lone dissenter was a Montana Congresswoman named Jeanette Rankin, the first woman elected to Congress. Rankin explained her decision: "As a woman I can't go to war, and I refuse to send anyone else." She had also voted against the United States' entry into World War I back in 1917.

53

THE JAPANESE ASSAULT

After their assault on Pearl Harbor, the Japanese attacked on a wide front across Southeast Asia. They conquered American Philippines and Guam, British Malaya, Burma, and Hong Kong, and the Dutch East Indies. Their forces captured numerous islands in the South Pacific. The Japanese plan was to construct a secure island border defended by naval and air power.

Attacking Australia

On February 19, 1942, 242 Japanese aircraft attacked the northern Australian city of Darwin. Ninety-seven further attacks against Australian cities and airbases continued until late 1943. Japan even used midget submarines to attack shipping in Sydney Harbour, sinking a troop ship on June 1, 1942.

Australia Bombing of Darwin 1942 45c

Australian stamp showing the bombing of Darwin in 1942.

FAST FACT!

In six months, Japan chased all European and American powers out of Southeast Asia.

The Fall of Singapore

Singapore was the largest British naval base in Southeast Asia. The Japanese advanced down through the jungles of Malaya to attack the base from the north. HMS *Prince of Wales* and HMS *Repulse*, sent by the British to stop the Japanese, were both sunk at sea. After eight days of bombardment and assault, the base fell to the Japanese. More than 80,000 British, Indian, and Australian troops were taken captive, the largest surrender of British military personnel in history.

Japanese aircraft sank HMS Prince of Wales off the coast of Malaysia in December 1941.

Canadians Fight

Canadians were heavily involved in the defense of the British colony of Hong Kong. In October 1941, 1,975 soldiers of the Royal Rifles of Canada and Winnipeg Grenadiers sailed from Vancouver to Hong Kong. During the fighting against the Japanese in December 1941, 290 Canadians were killed and 493 wounded. Many were taken as prisoners of war and forced to live in appalling conditions. A further 264 men died while in captivity.

Japanese soldiers invading the city of Hong Kong in 1941.

1942: THE TIDE BEGINS TO TURN

This was the year that the tide of war began to turn in the Allies' favor. At the start of 1942, the Axis powers swept through Asia, Europe, and North Africa. By the end of the year, the Allies had stopped the Japanese in the Pacific and the Germans at Stalingrad, and defeated the Axis in North Africa. The world war was changing.

German prisoners wait for transport after El Alamein.

Key Events

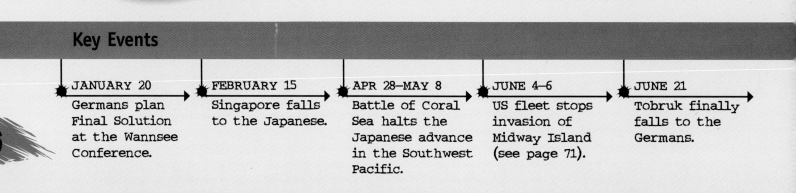

JANUARY 20	FEBRUARY 15	APR 28–MAY 8	JUNE 4–6	JUNE 21
Germans plan Final Solution at the Wannsee Conference.	Singapore falls to the Japanese.	Battle of Coral Sea halts the Japanese advance in the Southwest Pacific.	US fleet stops invasion of Midway Island (see page 71).	Tobruk finally falls to the Germans.

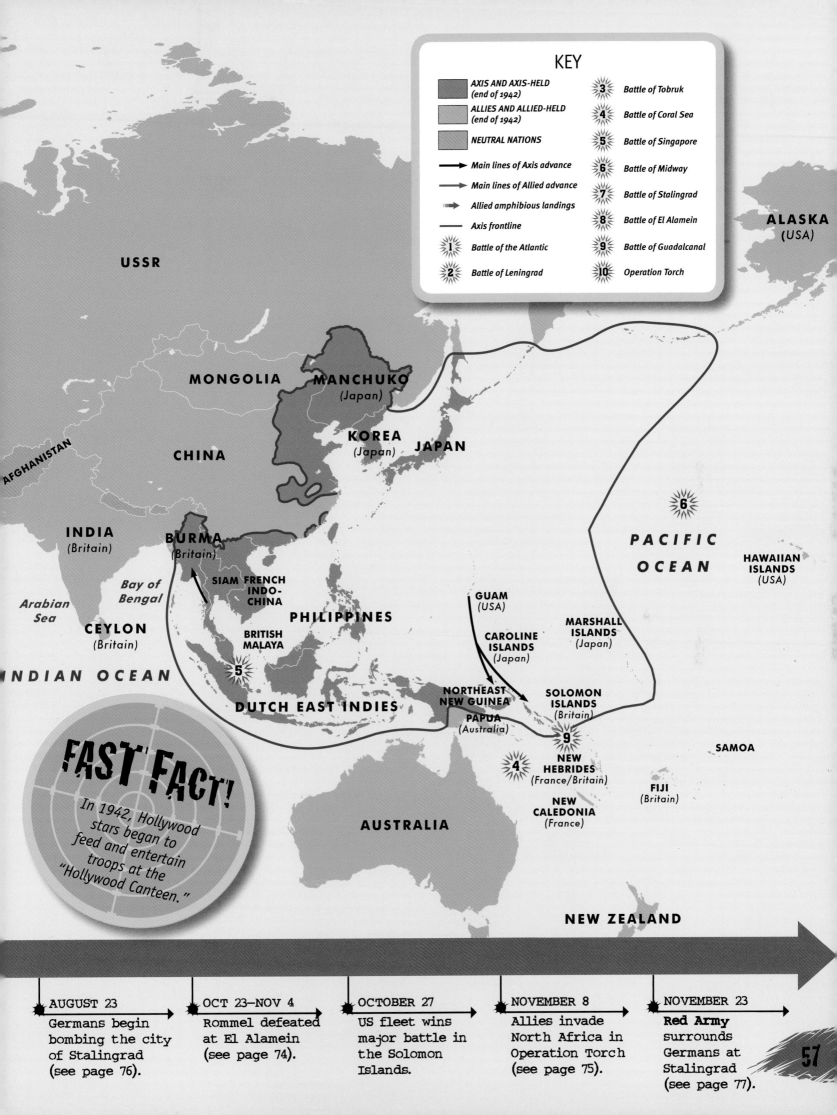

KEY

■	AXIS AND AXIS-HELD (end of 1942)
■	ALLIES AND ALLIED-HELD (end of 1942)
■	NEUTRAL NATIONS
→	Main lines of Axis advance
→	Main lines of Allied advance
⇢	Allied amphibious landings
—	Axis frontline
1	Battle of the Atlantic
2	Battle of Leningrad

3	Battle of Tobruk
4	Battle of Coral Sea
5	Battle of Singapore
6	Battle of Midway
7	Battle of Stalingrad
8	Battle of El Alamein
9	Battle of Guadalcanal
10	Operation Torch

USSR

ALASKA (USA)

MONGOLIA

MANCHUKO (Japan)

KOREA (Japan)

JAPAN

CHINA

AFGHANISTAN

INDIA (Britain)

BURMA (Britain)

SIAM

FRENCH INDO-CHINA

PHILIPPINES

Bay of Bengal

Arabian Sea

CEYLON (Britain)

BRITISH MALAYA

INDIAN OCEAN

DUTCH EAST INDIES

5

PACIFIC OCEAN

6

HAWAIIAN ISLANDS (USA)

GUAM (USA)

CAROLINE ISLANDS (Japan)

MARSHALL ISLANDS (Japan)

NORTHEAST NEW GUINEA

SOLOMON ISLANDS (Britain)

PAPUA (Australia)

9

SAMOA

4

NEW HEBRIDES (France/Britain)

FIJI (Britain)

NEW CALEDONIA (France)

AUSTRALIA

FAST FACT!

In 1942, Hollywood stars began to feed and entertain troops at the "Hollywood Canteen."

NEW ZEALAND

AUGUST 23
Germans begin bombing the city of Stalingrad (see page 76).

OCT 23–NOV 4
Rommel defeated at El Alamein (see page 74).

OCTOBER 27
US fleet wins major battle in the Solomon Islands.

NOVEMBER 8
Allies invade North Africa in Operation Torch (see page 75).

NOVEMBER 23
Red Army surrounds Germans at Stalingrad (see page 77).

FRANKLIN DELANO ROOSEVELT

When World War II began, President Franklin Roosevelt was already well on his way to successfully leading the United States out of the Great Depression. First elected in 1932, he won reelection in 1936, and again in 1940, as the war in Europe raged. Roosevelt was overwhelmingly reelected in 1944 to an unprecedented fourth term, but died in office in April 1945, just as the war in Europe was about to end.

Famous 1944 reelection poster. Uncle Sam points at F.D.R. and tells him to "stay and finish the job."

Bracing His Nation for War

President Roosevelt's inaugural speech of January 1941 stressed America's need to prepare for war: "In the face of great perils never before encountered, our strong purpose is to protect and to perpetuate the integrity of democracy. For this we muster the spirit of America . . ."

FAST FACT!
President Roosevelt was paralyzed from the waist down. He drove a specially adapted automobile which could be operated without the use of his legs.

The Infamy Speech

With America's entry into the war in 1941, Roosevelt proved to be a strong-willed and reassuring wartime leader. He gave weekly "fireside chats" over the radio which helped inspire and soothe millions of Americans. One of the defining moments of his presidency came the day after the Japanese attack on Pearl Harbor, when he made his famous "Infamy" radio speech.

"Yesterday, Dec 7, 1941—a date which will live in infamy—the United States of America was suddenly and deliberately attacked by naval and air forces of the Empire of Japan . . . I ask that the Congress declare that since the unprovoked and dastardly attack by Japan on Sunday, Dec 7, a state of war has existed between the United States and the Japanese empire."

—President Roosevelt, Dec. 8, 1941

Franklin Roosevelt during one of his "fireside chats," September 1941.

Roosevelt with soldiers in a mess hall, April 1945.

LIFE ON THE HOME FRONT

World War II was a total conflict that affected not only those on the front lines, but also the people at home. In some countries, every aspect of daily life was affected. In the United States, food was rationed, and factories began to turn out bombs and other wartime materials. Everybody worked hard to win the war.

Women at War

American women played a vital role during the war. Besides the many thousands who worked in factories, about 350,000 American women served in uniform. They served both in the United States and overseas, as volunteers for units such as the Women's Army Corps (WACS), the Navy Women's Reserve (WAVES), the Marine Corps Women's Reserve (MCWR), the Coast Guard Women's Reserve (SPARS), the Women Airforce Service Pilots (WASPS), the Army Nurse Corps, and the Navy Nurse Corps.

Wartime poster showing a women canning food and supporting rationing.

"OF COURSE I CAN!"

I'm patriotic as can be—
And ration points won't worry me!"

Rationing

Food was rationed in most countries because food could not be imported from abroad. People were issued with ration books that allowed them certain quantities of food each week. The ration was not high, but few people starved until the last months of the war in Europe. Governments encouraged people to grow their own food and suggested new recipes using odd ingredients, such as ground acorns instead of coffee.

Some victory gardeners showing their fine vegetables. 1942-1943.

Victory Gardens

Farm crops in the US were needed to provide food for troops, so the government encouraged citizens to plant vegetables in their backyards to help the war effort. The public embraced the idea, and more than 20 million people participated. Whether a precious few square feet of plantable dirt in the midst of a large city, or a sprawling yard in rural areas, people grew victory gardens. Everything from tomatoes to squash to beans and peas was grown across the country, putting extra food on the table and easing the impact of decreased meat and other rationed items.

FAST FACT!

With limited amounts of meat, butter, and sugar available, recipes of the day encouraged the consumer to use substitutes.

Two Daytona Beach, Florida, housewives welding in an aircraft construction class.

WARTIME PRODUCTION

WWII Poster boosting morale of American women contributing to the war effort.

Starting in December 1941, the United States had to quickly shift gears and change into wartime production mode. During the war, many private factories were converted to military production. All available equipment was needed to produce everything from food to clothing to weapons. One factory in Wisconsin went from making tissues to making machine-gun mounts.

Women working in a factory polishing the nose cones of airplanes.

"Every combat division, every naval task force, every squadron of fighting planes is dependent for its equipment and ammunition, and fuel and food . . . on the American people in civilian clothes, in the offices and in the factories, and on the farms at home."

—President Roosevelt, July 1943

Production of munitions in the United States

- 41,000,000,000 rounds of ammunition
- 310,000 aircraft
- 124,000 ships (all types)
- 100,000 tanks and armoured vehicles
- 6 million tons of bombs

War Bonds

The government needed lots of money to pay for the war. Selling bonds to Americans was a way for the United States to quickly get money (which would be paid back later, with interest). During the war, movie stars made special appearances to help convince the public to buy bonds.

No More Cars

On February 1, 1942 the US government shut down automobile production. Materials used to make cars were now needed to create tanks, bombers, and aircraft carriers. The only automobile companies to continue producing during the war were Willys and American Bantam, who made the versatile Army vehicle known as the Jeep. Normal production resumed in 1946.

Wartime Jeep production at an auto plant, in Toledo, Ohio.

FAST FACT!

Between 1942 and 1945, the United States produced more than double the number of airplanes as any other country.

THE HOLOCAUST

In 1942, senior Nazis met near Lake Wannsee in Berlin to plan the "Final Solution to the Jewish problem." The Jewish people were to be exterminated. Historians call this the **"Holocaust"** from the Greek words: holos ("whole") and kaustós ("burned"). It resulted in the murder of around six million Jewish men, women, and children. The Nazis did not act alone. They were helped by people from within the European countries they occupied.

What Hitler Believed

Hitler believed that Jews were contaminating the purity of the German race. He also blamed them for Germany's economic problems and for losing World War I.

Persecution of the Jews

Persecution of the Jews began almost immediately after Hitler took power. By the time the war started, a lot of suffering had already been inflicted. After 1939, Jews were rounded up and made to live in ghettos (specially designated, very crowded areas within a city), or concentration or labor camps. Many more were shot or gassed in mobile gas vans.

German Anti-Semitic poster. "Der ist Schuld am Kriege!" translates to "The war is his fault!" It shows a finger pointing accusingly at a Jewish man wearing a yellow star, which all Jews were forced to wear.

Death Camps

By 1943, the focus of the camps shifted from imprisonment and labor to death—most who arrived were immediately killed in gas chambers. Concentration camps operated in occupied countries, including Austria, France, Latvia, Estonia, Poland, Lithuania, and Yugoslavia. One of the most notorious camps was Auschwitz-Birkenau, where more than one million prisoners were killed.

Children at Auschwitz wearing the infamous striped concentration camp uniforms.

FAST FACT!

Jewish people call the Holocaust the "Shoah," which means "catastrophe" or "destruction."

The Death Toll

As well as Jews, many millions of other people were also imprisoned, enslaved, and murdered at the hands of the Nazis.

- 5.9 million Jews
- More than 200,000 Roma (gypsies)
- 250,000 disabled people
- 15,000 homosexuals
- 5,000 Jehovah's witnesses

Saving the Jews

Many Jewish people were saved by acts of bravery carried out by both Jewish and non-Jewish people. Oskar Schindler, whose factory in Poland made equipment essential to the German army, presented the Germans with a list of 1,200 Jewish workers he said were needed in his factory. "Schindler's List" saved Jewish lives. Other heroes were the Swedish diplomat Raoul Wallenberg and the Swiss diplomat Carl Lutz, who issued papers giving Jews the official protection of their respective neutral countries.

BOMBING GERMANY

The British, and later, the Americans, bombed German cities, just as the Germans bombed cities during the Blitz. Day and night, fleets of bombers escorted by fighters headed east to Germany to rain down destruction on its towns and cities.

Hamburg

On April 8, 1942, 272 British bombers attacked Hamburg, but the resulting damage was nothing compared to a raid that took place a year later. Over ten nights starting on July 24, 1943, the RAF and the US Air Force bombed the city of Hamburg—a major port and industrial center. The dry conditions led to a firestorm with winds of up to 150 mph and temperatures in excess of 1,500°F. More than 34,000 civilians were killed, 37,000 wounded, and many buildings totally destroyed.

"We are all alright, but every night you feel the threat and want to stay awake. Many people in Hamburg are spending the nights in the air raid shelters, but that is very stressful."

—letter from Hamburg family, August 1943

FAST FACT!

No one knows the exact tally, but about 350,000 people were killed during the bombing of Germany.

Dresden

One of the most controversial raids took place against Dresden on February 13–15, 1945. Dresden was an important rail center used by German troops and was in the way of Russian troops fighting their way to Berlin. However, the bombs mainly hit civilian targets. More than 25,000 people were killed and the ancient city destroyed.

German refugees wait with their belongings in Berlin's Anhalter Station, 1945.

The greater part of Dresden was destroyed during the Allied air raids on the city.

The Bombing War

Just as the Blitz failed to shake the morale of British people, the Allied attacks failed to shake the Germans. The campaign was criticized for targeting civilian instead of industrial or military targets. The Allied bombers did have some spectacular successes. On May 16, 1943, the British 617 Squadron used bouncing bombs to destroy two large dams that flooded the Ruhr valley and the heart of German industry.

UNDER OCCUPATION

During the war, many countries were occupied by the Axis. Some people welcomed their new rulers and collaborated with them. Others resisted their occupiers. Where no one would collaborate, the Axis imposed its own military rulers. In all occupied countries, people were forced to work for the Axis, producing food, weapons, and other materials for the war effort.

French resistance fighters learn how to use their guns. They were very brave and risked certain death if captured by the enemy.

Collaboration

In unoccupied France, General Pétain led a government of **collaboration** that supported the Germans. In Norway, a Nazi sympathizer named Vidkun Quisling became prime minister, while a pro-fascist government ruled Croatia.

Resistance

Resistance groups were formed across Europe to resist Axis rule. The most effective were those in countries where the landscape was wild enough to hide in, such as Norway, Yugoslavia, France, and Greece. Many groups had great success, carrying out acts of sabotage and sending intelligence back to the Allies.

68

Partisans

Partisans were **guerrilla** armies fighting mainly German troops. The most successful partisans were in Yugoslavia. Led by Josip Broz Tito, the partisans managed to drive the Germans out of Yugoslavia by the end of 1944. In Italy, partisans managed to capture and kill the former Italian leader, Benito Mussolini. Partisans operating behind German lines in the USSR wrecked 18,000 trains and killed, wounded, or imprisoned thousands of German troops.

Japanese Rule

In Europe, Germany and Italy occupied independent nations. In Asia, however, Japan mainly occupied European or American colonies, whose people saw the Japanese as liberators from colonial rule. The Japanese used local leaders to run these countries and gave both Burma and the Philippines limited independence. All the occupied countries joined the Great East Asia Co-Prosperity Sphere to promote regional cooperation. However, the Japanese retained full control.

Japanese soldiers march in Burma as Rangoon falls.

Russian countrywomen working in the fields for the German Army.

BATTLES IN THE PACIFIC

After Pearl Harbor, the Japanese quickly conquered large parts of East Asia and many Pacific islands. Their assault was halted in the summer of 1942 by the world's first battle between aircraft carriers in the Coral Sea and then by two defeats at Midway Island and Guadalcanal. These were the first Allied victories against Japan.

USS Wasp after an attack by enemy submarines while escorting ships and supplies at Guadalcanal in the Solomon Islands.

Survivors of the sinking of the US aircraft carrier Lexington climb aboard another ship following the Battle of the Coral Sea.

The Coral Sea

On May 3–4, 1942, the Japanese seized Tulagi in the Solomon Islands. Aware that an American fleet was nearby, the Japanese fleet sailed south into the Coral Sea to fight it. The two carrier fleets never met, their planes fighting over great distances. Neither side won the battle, although the Japanese were forced to call off their invasion of Port Moresby in New Guinea.

Battle of Midway

On June 4–7, 1942, the Japanese and American navies met halfway across the Pacific Ocean at Midway Island. The Japanese wanted to capture this island, which was close to the vital US naval base in Hawaii. American codebreakers found out the date of the attack, allowing their fleet to lure the Japanese into a trap. After heavy fighting, the Americans won. After Midway, the Japanese news announced a great victory. Only Emperor Hirohito and the highest naval commanders were told the truth.

The Navajos

The Native American Navajo language is very complex and at the start of the war had not even been written down. US forces in the Pacific used Navajo speakers to code and decode secret military messages. It took them 20 seconds to encode, transmit, and decode a three-line English message as opposed to 30 minutes by machine.

Native American Navajo sending coded messages over a field radio in the South Pacific.

Guadalcanal

Some of the most intense fighting took place in Guadalcanal in the Solomon Islands. The Japanese seized the island in July 1942 and built an airstrip that threatened Australia. US Marines seized the airstrip in August 1942, but had to fight the Japanese for a further six months before they took control of the whole island. It was one of the bloodiest victories in the entire war.

American troops unloading supplies and equipment from landing craft at Guadalcanal.

71

EL ALAMEIN

The see-saw battle between the British Commonwealth and Axis forces in North Africa came to a climax in November 1942, when General Montgomery, commander of the British 8th Army, defeated General Rommel's Panzer Afrika Korps. It was one of the greatest British victories of the war.

A British Crusader Mk 1 tank advancing in the desert during the Battle of El Alamein.

The Battle

After the fall of Tobruk in June 1942, Rommel pushed the British back into Egypt. Secret intelligence allowed the British to destroy Axis supply ships. This meant Rommel's army only had three days' supply of fuel. Montgomery built up his strength, then struck on October 23, achieving victory by November 11.

General Rommel (left) with his troops in the desert near El Alamein, Nov. 1942.

Malta

The British island of Malta lay in the middle of the supply line between Italy and the Axis forces in North Africa. Axis aircraft continuously bombed the island from June 1940 to November 1942, yet it did not surrender. Malta was awarded the George Cross by King George, an honor for bravery and heroism normally intended for civilians but in this case awarded to an entire island. Malta was so proud of this honor that they incorporated the cross into their flag.

War graves at the Commonwealth Cemetery in El Alamein, Egypt.

ROMMEL VS. MONTGOMERY

Rommel's Panzer Army
- 116,000 men
- 547 tanks
- 552 artillery pieces
- 480 aircraft

Montgomery's 8th Army
- 195,000 men
- 1,029 tanks
- 908 artillery pieces
- 530 aircraft

The Cemetery at El Alamein

Where were World War II's combat dead buried? Often, they were buried near the battlefield where they fell. At the El Alamein Cemetery, for example, are 7,342 graves (mainly British subjects) of those who died in El Alamein and other Northern Africa locations. Of those, 815 are unidentified.

OPERATION TORCH

While the British and Commonwealth forces were winning at El Alamein in northeast Africa, a joint American, British, and Free French force landed in northwest Africa. Just six months later, the whole of North Africa was cleared of Axis troops and the invasion of Europe could begin. In 1942, the USSR demanded that the Allies open a second front against Germany in western Europe to relieve pressure on the Russian army in the east. The Americans agreed, but the British proposed to invade North Africa and secure the Mediterranean before invading mainland Europe.

FAST FACT!

The operation to invade North Africa was originally called Operation Gymnast.

The Pincer

As Allied troops moved east toward Tunisia, the British 8th Army headed west from El Alamein. The plan was to "pinch" the Axis troops from both sides in a "pincer" movement. The plan worked. 240,000 Axis troops were caught at Tunis and surrendered on May 13, 1943. It was a massive blow to the German war effort.

Axis soldiers who were taken prisoner in 1943.

Changed His Tune

The commander of the Germans' 90th Light African Division, Major General Theodor Graf Von Sponeck, was told by the Allies that he must surrender unconditionally. He proclaimed he would fight to the last bullet . . . and then after some thought surrendered to the British 8th Army's New Zealand Division!

Allied troops landing in North Africa during Operation Torch.

Operation Torch

From November 8–16, 1942, 107,000 Allied troops in three task forces landed in French Morocco (near Casablanca) and Algeria (near Oran and near Algiers). The invasion force was led by American General Dwight Eisenhower. Vichy French forces in control of the two colonies fought back but were soon defeated. Admiral Darlan, former deputy leader of **Vichy France**, was in Algeria at the time and quickly arranged a ceasefire. In response, German troops entered Vichy France and occupied the whole country.

Anti-aircraft fire lighting up the sky during an Allied raid on Algiers.

STALINGRAD

FAST FACT!

In 1925, Tsaritsyn was renamed Stalingrad after the Soviet leader— Joseph Stalin.

The most brutal battle of the war was waged over control of the industrial city of Stalingrad in southwest Russia. The battle lasted for more than six months before the Germans were defeated. When it was over, the tide of war had turned decisively in favor of the Soviets, and their Allies.

The Red Army in house-to-house battles in Stalingrad.

The Titanic Battle

The Axis:
- 1,040,000 men
- 10,250 artillery pieces
- 500 tanks
- 402 aircraft

The Soviet Red Army:
- 1,143,000 men
- 13,451 artillery pieces
- 900 tanks
- 1,115 aircraft

The Battle

On 23 August, 1942, the Germans began bombing the city. By mid-November they had pushed the Russians back to a narrow strip of buildings along the west bank of the Volga River. On November 19, the Soviet Red Army launched Operation Uranus that encircled the Germans and cut off their escape routes. Hitler insisted his troops stay on and fight. Without food and ammunition, the German Sixth Army surrendered on February 2, 1943.

Close Fighting

The fighting for control of Stalingrad was so intense that snipers from one side shot at enemy troops fighting back from the next floor of the same building. Russian snipers were given medals for their work. One sniper, Vasily Zaytsev, is thought to have killed 225 Germans between November 10 and December 17, 1942.

Fighting in the ruins of the battered city.

Casualties

THE AXIS
850,000 men killed, wounded, or captured

THE RUSSIANS
1,129,610 killed or wounded

German prisoners taken by the Soviets at the end of the battle. Few would survive the harsh conditions in captivity.

Total Defeat

Approximately 91,000 Germans were taken prisoner after Stalingrad. Only around 5,000 of them would survive captivity to return home.

1943: A FOOTHOLD IN EUROPE

After the catastrophic German defeat at Stalingrad, the course of the war turned decisively in favor of the Allies. Russian troops pushed steadily westward, fighting and winning major battles at Kursk and elsewhere. In July, the Allies opened up a second front in Europe and invaded Italy, which soon surrendered. In the Pacific, the Americans began to attack the Japanese.

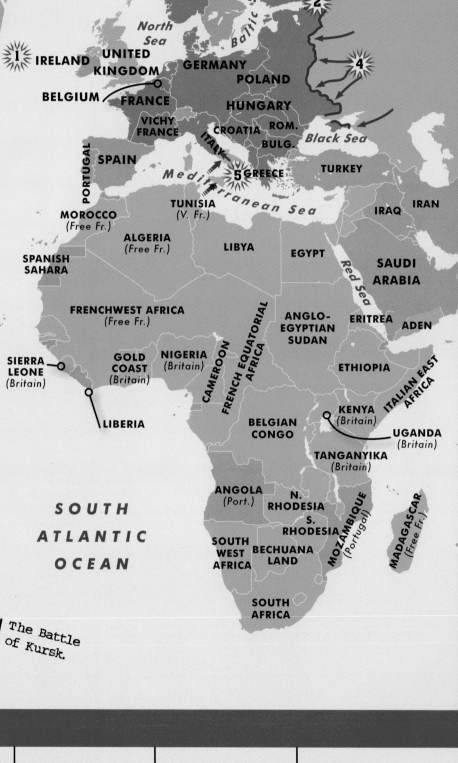

ARCTIC OCEAN

NORWAY
SWEDEN
FINLAND
Baltic Sea
North Sea
IRELAND
UNITED KINGDOM
GERMANY
POLAND
BELGIUM
FRANCE
HUNGARY
VICHY FRANCE
CROATIA
ROM.
ITALY
BULG.
Black Sea
SPAIN
GREECE
TURKEY
PORTUGAL
Mediterranean Sea
TUNISIA (V. Fr.)
IRAQ
IRAN
MOROCCO (Free Fr.)
ALGERIA (Free Fr.)
LIBYA
EGYPT
Red Sea
SAUDI ARABIA
SPANISH SAHARA
FRENCH WEST AFRICA (Free Fr.)
ANGLO-EGYPTIAN SUDAN
ERITREA
ADEN
SIERRA LEONE (Britain)
GOLD COAST (Britain)
NIGERIA (Britain)
CAMEROON
FRENCH EQUATORIAL AFRICA
ETHIOPIA
ITALIAN EAST AFRICA
LIBERIA
BELGIAN CONGO
KENYA (Britain)
UGANDA (Britain)
TANGANYIKA (Britain)
SOUTH ATLANTIC OCEAN
ANGOLA (Port.)
N. RHODESIA
S. RHODESIA
MOZAMBIQUE (Portugal)
MADAGASCAR (Free Fr.)
SOUTH WEST AFRICA
BECHUANA LAND
SOUTH AFRICA

The Battle of Kursk.

Key Events

JANUARY 21–24	FEBRUARY 2	MAY 13	MAY 16	JUNE 30
Allies demand **unconditional surrender** of the Axis.	Germans surrender at Stalingrad.	Axis armies surrender in North Africa.	Germans crush Jewish uprising in Warsaw ghetto.	US starts Operation Cartwheel against Japanese (see page 86).

KEY

■	**AXIS AND AXIS-HELD** (end of 1943)	── Axis frontline
■	**ALLIES AND ALLIED-HELD** (end of 1943)	✶**1** Battle of the Atlantic
■	**NEUTRAL NATIONS**	✶**2** Battle of Leningrad
→	Main lines of Axis advance	✶**3** Operation Cartwheel
→	Main lines of Allied advance	✶**4** Kursk
⇢	Allied amphibious landings	✶**5** Italy

ALASKA (USA)

USSR

MONGOLIA   MANCHUKO (Japan)

CHINA   KOREA (Japan)   JAPAN

ANISTAN

INDIA (Britain)   BURMA (Britain)

SIAM   FRENCH INDO-CHINA

Bay of Bengal

PACIFIC OCEAN

HAWAIIAN ISLANDS (USA)

rabian Sea

CEYLON (Britain)

PHILIPPINES

BRITISH MALAYA

GUAM (USA)

CAROLINE ISLANDS (Japan)

MARSHALL ISLANDS (Japan)

INDIAN OCEAN

DUTCH EAST INDIES

NORTHEAST NEW GUINEA

SOLOMON ISLANDS (Britain) ✶**3**

PAPUA (Australia)

NEW HEBRIDES (France/Britain)

SAMOA

FIJI (Britain)

NEW CALEDONIA (France)

FAST FACT!

The number of German U-boats sunk by the Allies went up from 86 in 1942 to 240 in 1943.

AUSTRALIA

NEW ZEALAND

JULY 4–15
Russia wins major tank battle at Kursk (see page 81).

JULY 9
Allies invade Sicily (see page 84).

SEPTEMBER 8
Italian government surrenders to the Allies.

SEPTEMBER 10
German troops occupy Rome.

DECEMBER 1
Three Allied leaders meet in Tehran to discuss war strategy (see page 89).

KURSK

German soldiers sat on top of an assault gun III at the Battle of Kursk.

Everything about the battle of Kursk was massive. There were almost 3 million soldiers involved, 8,000 tanks, 35,000 guns and mortars, and 190 miles of Soviet defenses behind the front line. About 300,000 civilians helped build Soviet defenses. Kursk was the biggest tank battle ever fought in history. It was the first time in the war that the Russian Red Army stopped a German offensive in its tracks.

Tanks

Soviet T-34:
- 45–47mm front armor
- 76.2mm main gun plus 2 machine guns
- 26.5 tons weight
- 4 crew

German Panther:
- 15–120mm front armor
- 75mm main gun plus 2 machine guns
- 44.8 tons weight
- 5 crew

FAST FACT!

More than 70 percent of all German tanks and 65 percent of its aircraft fought at Kursk.

The Battlefield

By mid-1943, a huge Russian kink in the front line pushed westward out into the German front line. On July 5, the Germans attacked the kink in order to straighten out the front line, but the Russians were ready for them and prepared lines of defenses. A big Russian counter-offensive began on July 12 that pushed the Germans back, capturing German-held territory along an extensive battle front until the battle ended on August 23.

During the Battle of Kursk.

The Germans and Russians fought the biggest ever tank battle at Kursk in July 1943.

Changing Fortunes

The battles of Stalingrad and Kursk marked a critical moment in the war. Up to then, the Germans had the best army with the best equipment. The Russians had been unprepared for war and had been overwhelmed by the Germans. Now the situation changed completely. The Russians had the best-equipped army and were highly motivated to fight. The Germans were outgunned and were exhausted from fighting both the Russians in the east, and the Anglo-American forces in the west.

THE DRAFT

In September 1940, President Franklin Roosevelt signed the Selective Training and Service Act, which required all men between the ages of 21 and 35 to register for the draft. It was the first peacetime draft in United States' history. By the end of the war, six draft registrations had been held and 10 million men had been inducted into the military.

Franklin Roosevelt signing the Burke-Wadsworth Conscription Act, September 16, 1940.

Lottery

The government selected men through a lottery system. Each man who registered was assigned a number by the draft board. Then, numbers from 1–7,836 were placed in a giant glass bowl and drawn one by one. Whoever around the country had that number had to report for induction. The first number drawn was 158, which was held by 6,175 men.

Two US soldiers draw numbers for the draft lottery.

Old Man's Registration

After the United States entered the war, a new selective service act made men between 18 and 45 liable for military service. On April 27, 1942, The Fourth Draft Registration, or "Old Man's Registration" called for all men aged 45–65 to register for the draft. This registration was not intended to find men for military service, but to get an inventory of manpower that could be used for the war effort.

Conscientious Objectors

Those who objected to fighting in the war on religious or other personal grounds could serve in the medical corps or perform other war-related services. A total of 72,354 men applied for conscientious objector status during the war.

Camp Marietta: the quarters of Ohio's conscientious objectors.

FAST FACT!

About 60% of those who served during WWII were draftees, while 40% were volunteers.

Jobs Would Wait

Men who were drafted would be leaving their regular civilian jobs to enter the military for a year or longer. The Selective Training and Service Act said that their employers had to rehire them once they were discharged "unless the employer's circumstances have so changed as to make it impossible or unreasonable to do so."

THE INVASION OF ITALY

Ever since the German invasion of Russia in June 1941, the Russians had asked their western allies to launch a new front against Germany in Western Europe to take some of the pressure off their own front line. By July 1943, the western Allies were ready to invade Italy.

Quick Successes

Allied airborne troops landed in Sicily on July 9, and soon conquered the island. On July 25, Mussolini was overthrown and the new Italian government asked for an armistice or truce with the Allies, which was signed on September 3. Allied troops landed in Italy on the same day and by September 8, Italy had surrendered. Two days later, German troops occupied Rome and freed Mussolini from prison. Mussolini was then installed as head of the new Italian Social Republic, known as the Salò Republic from the town where it was based. The Germans continued to fight the Allies up the length of Italy.

Residents of Palermo, Sicily, line the streets to greet US tanks after the town had surrendered to the Allies.

Monte Cassino

One of the biggest battles took place around the monastery of Monte Cassino. In February 1944, the Allies bombed the monastery, which was then occupied by the Germans. There they remained under constant bombardment until the Polish army managed to evict them in May 1944. Casualties numbered more than 75,000 and the monastery, which dated back to the year 529 AD, was destroyed.

A New Zealand anti-tank gun crew in action at the Battle of Monte Cassino.

The ruins of the abbey of Monte Cassino.

The End of Mussolini

After the surrender of Italy, many Italians formed partisan groups and joined the Allies in fighting the Germans. On April 27, 1945, partisans stopped Mussolini and his mistress—Clara Petacci—as they were fleeing into exile in Switzerland. The next day, Mussolini and Petacci were executed in a square in Milan.

OPERATION CARTWHEEL

Despite their setbacks at Midway and Guadalcanal, the Japanese still occupied New Guinea and the Solomon Islands in the South Pacific. However, the Americans had a bigger navy and superior air power. This inspired a clever strategy to clear the islands of Japanese forces.

American assault boat carrying Marines to the beach in the Northern Solomons.

FAST FACT!

Most Japanese soldiers would not surrender, preferring to fight to the death.

Operation Cartwheel

US Operation Cartwheel targeted ten different island groups, which were slowly cleared of Japanese forces one by one in a cartwheel action between June 1943 and March 1944. Slowly, this cartwheel action took the Americans closer to Japan itself.

Clearing Rabaul

One of the main purposes behind Operation Cartwheel was the destruction of a major Japanese military base located at Rabaul on the Pacific island of New Britain. Not only was the base interfering with communications between the United States and Australia, its strategic position was preventing Allied advances toward the Philippines.

Operation Vengeance

The Americans blamed the Japanese admiral Isoroku Yamamoto for the 1941 raid on Pearl Harbor. On April 18, 1943, they used intelligence about his movements to shoot down his transport aircraft over Bougainville Island (one of the Solomon Islands). His death severely damaged Japanese morale.

Battle of the Philippine Sea

In 1944, American forces swept through the islands of the central Pacific toward the Philippines. On June 19–20, the Japanese and American carrier fleets met in the Philippine Sea. The Americans won a decisive victory, sinking three Japanese carriers and downing 645 planes. The Japanese navy never recovered from this defeat. In October, US forces began the invasion of the Philippines themselves.

The USS *Kitkun Bay* prepares its fighters during the Battle of the Philippine Sea.

THE BIG THREE

With the entry of the United States into the war in 1941, the Allies now consisted of three powerful nations. Britain, the USSR, and the US. Although they met up separately on a number of occasions, all three of the **Big Three** leaders only met together three times. These meetings helped decide the course of the war.

FAST FACT!

President Roosevelt hoped to get Stalin to accept Democratic principles.

Churchill and Roosevelt

The British and American leaders met regularly during the war, and became close friends. In August 1941, they met aboard the USS *Augusta* in Placentia Bay off the coast of Newfoundland, Canada. They drafted a document called the Atlantic Charter, which listed eight common principles for the post-war world. They also met in Casablanca, Morocco, in January 1943, where they agreed to demand the unconditional surrender of the Axis powers. In other words, no negotiated peace, only total surrender.

Tehran

The first meeting of the Big Three took place in the Soviet embassy in Tehran, capital of Iran, from November 26 to December 1, 1943. The three leaders got to know each other and agreed on their overall objectives. Above all, the western Allies agreed to invade occupied France in 1944.

Yalta

With the end of the war in sight, the Big Three met in Yalta in the Crimea, Russia, in February 1945. The three leaders discussed and agreed on how the post-war reorganization of Europe would look.

Potsdam

Two months after the defeat of Germany, the Big Three met at Potsdam in the suburbs of Berlin in July 1945. Roosevelt had died and was replaced at the table by Harry Truman. Halfway through the conference, Winston Churchill was replaced by Clement Attlee after being defeated in the British general election. The Big Three agreed to divide Germany between their three countries and France.

German stamp marking the 25th anniversary of the Potsdam Conference.

25
DDR

25 JAHRE POTSDAMER ABKOMMEN

89

TUSKEGEE AIRMEN

Tuskegee Airmen. The first American all-black pilot unit.

Though African-Americans made up 13 percent of US military manpower during World War I, there were no black pilots in the armed forces. In the years that followed, despite efforts to enlist for pilot training, African-Americans were not accepted. This finally changed as World War II began, with a military pilot training program that was begun at the Tuskegee Institute in Alabama. Over 1,000 pilots were trained there during the war.

It Started with a Bill

In 1939, a bill was enacted that said the government would support the training of African-American pilots by lending equipment to schools that offered flight training for them. It was a start, but did not guarantee acceptance into the military. Roosevelt wanted this to change, and pushed for the Air Corps to accept applications from black pilots. They finally did in 1941.

Minorities in the US Military during World War II

African Americans: 901,896
Puerto Rican: 51,438
Japanese American: 33,000
Native American: 20,000
Chinese American: 13,311
Filipino American: 11,506
Hawaiian: 1,320

The First Airmen

The first Tuskegee aviation class with 13 cadets began on July 19, 1941. Five graduated in March 1942. General George Stratemeyer, in his speech to the first graduating class, said: "I am sure that everyone present, senses that this graduation is an historic moment, filled with portent of great good."

Segregation

Despite being offered the chance to participate in the Air Corps, blacks were still segregated. An official White House statement in 1940, encouraged the training of African American pilots, but said: "The policy of the War Department is not to intermingle colored and white enlisted personnel."

Success in the Air

The Tuskegee Airmen flew more than 1,200 missions for the 99th, 100th, 301st, and 302nd Fighter Squadrons under the 12th Air Force. The 332nd Fighter Group flew at least 312 missions for the 15th Air Force. In total, they flew over 15,000 sorties and destroyed over 260 enemy airplanes. Tuskegee Airmen were awarded many honors, including the Distinguished Flying Cross, Legion of Merit, Silver star, Purple Heart, and the Croix de Guerre.

Cadets stand to attention at flight training school, Tuskegee, Alabama, March 1942.

9i

WARSAW GHETTO UPRISING

Isolating Jews in **ghettos** within cities was an early Nazi strategy. However, by 1942, the plan had changed, and Jews were now being deported en masse directly to concentration camps. By March 1943, more than 300,000 Jews had been forced out of the ghetto in Warsaw and deported to Treblinka. Beginning in April, a group of armed ghetto inhabitants led an armed revolt against the Nazis for 27 days. Though the uprising ended in defeat for the Jews, it was one of the war's most powerful and tragic acts.

1943: Fire breaks out during the Warsaw Ghetto Uprising, a Jewish insurrection against the German forces who had occupied Poland.

Statistics

Ghetto population in April 1943: 55,000-60,000
Resistance fighters: 750
Weapons: 17 rifles, some handguns, Molotov cocktails
Killed: 300 Germans, 7,000 Jews

The Uprising

The uprising was organized by two Polish resistance groups working together: the Jewish Combat Organization (Zydowska Organizacja Bojowa or ZOB) and the Jewish Military Union (Zydowski Zwiazek Wojskowy or ZZW). The uprising was led by a 23-year-old underground activist named Mordecai Anielewicz, who helped prepare and train the fighters. He was killed in his ghetto bunker on May 8th.

"Self-defense in the ghetto will have been a reality. Jewish armed resistance and revenge are facts. I have been a witness to the magnificent, heroic fighting of Jewish men in battle."

—Mordecai Anielewicz, April 23

Captured Jewish civilians who participated in the Warsaw Ghetto Uprising are marched out of the city by Nazi troops, Warsaw, Poland, April 19, 1943.

First Attempt

The uprising was preceded by an armed rebellion on January 18, 1943, when a group of armed Jews rebelled as they were being assembled for deportation. Most died, but the seeds were planted, and resistance fighters began to create bunkers in which to hide and make other preparations.

93

1944: EUROPE IS LIBERATED

During 1944, the three Axis powers were slowly driven out of their conquered territories in Europe and Asia. In June 1944, the Allies finally opened the second front against Nazi Germany by launching a massive seaborne invasion of France. After a slow start, the Allies raced across France toward the German border. The end of the war was in sight.

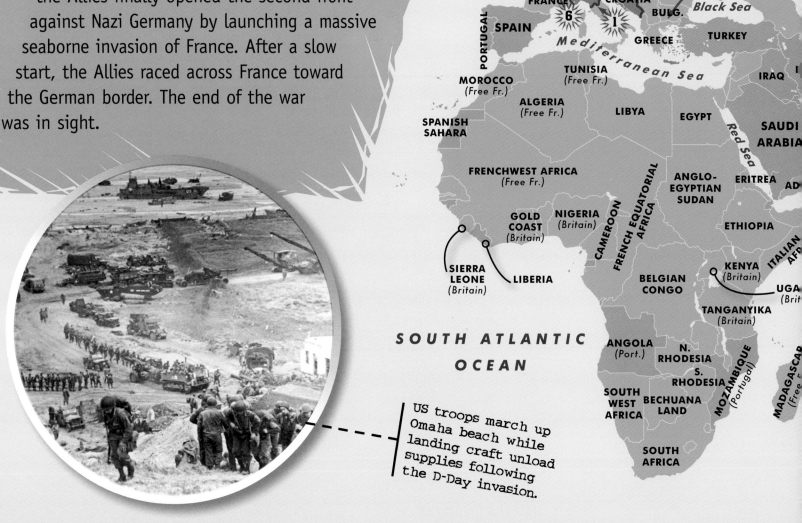

ARCTIC OCEAN

NORWAY
SWEDEN
FINLAND
North Sea
Baltic Sea
IRELAND
UNITED KINGDOM
GERMANY
POLAND
FRANCE
HUNGARY
VICHY FRANCE
ITALY
CROATIA
ROM.
BULG.
Black Sea
PORTUGAL
SPAIN
GREECE
TURKEY
Mediterranean Sea
MOROCCO (Free Fr.)
TUNISIA (Free Fr.)
IRAQ
ALGERIA (Free Fr.)
LIBYA
EGYPT
Red Sea
SAUDI ARABIA
SPANISH SAHARA
FRENCH WEST AFRICA (Free Fr.)
FRENCH EQUATORIAL AFRICA
ANGLO-EGYPTIAN SUDAN
ERITREA
GOLD COAST (Britain)
NIGERIA (Britain)
CAMEROON
ETHIOPIA
ITALIAN AFR.
SIERRA LEONE (Britain)
LIBERIA
KENYA (Britain)
UGA (Brit
BELGIAN CONGO
TANGANYIKA (Britain)
SOUTH ATLANTIC OCEAN
ANGOLA (Port.)
N. RHODESIA
S. RHODESIA
MOZAMBIQUE (Portugal)
MADAGASCAR (Free F
SOUTH WEST AFRICA
BECHUANA LAND
SOUTH AFRICA

US troops march up Omaha beach while landing craft unload supplies following the D-Day invasion.

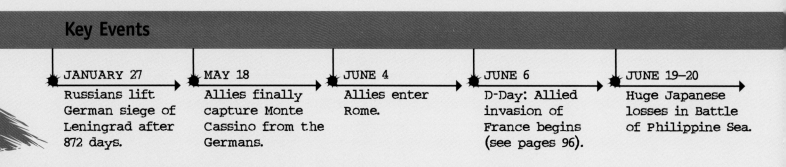

Key Events

JANUARY 27	MAY 18	JUNE 4	JUNE 6	JUNE 19–20
Russians lift German siege of Leningrad after 872 days.	Allies finally capture Monte Cassino from the Germans.	Allies enter Rome.	D-Day: Allied invasion of France begins (see pages 96).	Huge Japanese losses in Battle of Philippine Sea.

KEY

AXIS AND AXIS-HELD (end of 1944)

ALLIES AND ALLIED-HELD (end of 1944)

NEUTRAL NATIONS

→ Main lines of Axis advance

→ Main lines of Allied advance

⇢ Allied amphibious landings

— Axis frontline

1 Monte Cassino
2 Imphal
3 Operation Overlord
4 Philippines Sea
5 Operation Bagration
6 Operation Dragoon
7 Warsaw
8 Leyte Gulf
9 Battle of the Bulge

FAST FACT!

The D-Day landings on June 6 were the largest seaborne invasion in history.

USSR

ALASKA (USA)

MONGOLIA

MANCHUKO (Japan)

KOREA (Japan)

JAPAN

CHINA

AFGHANISTAN

INDIA (Britain)

2 BURMA (Britain)

SIAM

FRENCH INDO-CHINA

PHILIPPINES

4

8

GUAM (USA)

PACIFIC OCEAN

HAWAIIAN ISLANDS (USA)

Bay of Bengal

Arabian Sea

CEYLON (Britain)

BRITISH MALAYA

CAROLINE ISLANDS (Japan)

MARSHALL ISLANDS (Japan)

DUTCH EAST INDIES

NORTHEAST NEW GUINEA

PAPUA (Australia)

SOLOMON ISLANDS (Britain)

INDIAN OCEAN

NEW HEBRIDES (France/Britain)

SAMOA

FIJI (Britain)

NEW CALEDONIA (France)

AUSTRALIA

NEW ZEALAND

JULY 17
Russian Red Army crosses into Poland.

AUGUST 15
Allied troops land in southern France.

AUGUST 25
The French Resistance helps liberate Paris (see page 98).

SEPTEMBER 14
Allies liberate Belgium and reach German frontier.

DECEMBER 16
Germans launch final attack at the Battle of the Bulge (see page 112).

D-DAY

After a lengthy aerial and naval bombardment, and an airborne assault at midnight, Allied troops began to land on the beaches of Normandy. The first landing took place at 6:30 AM (known as H-Hour) on June 6, 1944 (known as D-Day). The Allied invasion of France had begun. The Second Front had at last opened up in Europe.

The Battle of Normandy, 1944.

Operation Overlord

Planning Operation Overlord (the codename for the Normandy invasion) began in 1943. A huge fleet of 6,939 ships was assembled from eight national navies, including 4,126 landing craft and 1,213 warships. Everything was ready to go on June 5, but due to bad weather the invasion was postponed a day.

Deception

The obvious place to invade France was across the narrowest part of the English Channel at Calais. In preparation, the Germans had heavily fortified this area. The Allies deceived them into believing the attack would take place here by pretending there was a large army waiting at Kent, directly across from Calais, to cross the Channel.

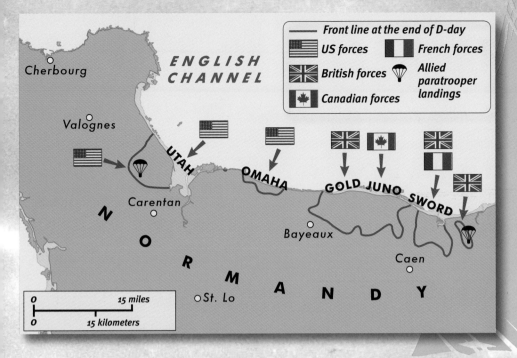

Front line at the end of D-day
US forces
British forces
Canadian forces
French forces
Allied paratrooper landings

ENGLISH CHANNEL

Cherbourg

Valognes

UTAH

OMAHA

GOLD JUNO SWORD

Carentan

NORMANDY

Bayeaux

Caen

St. Lo

0   15 miles
0   15 kilometers

The Beaches

The Allies codenamed five main Normandy beaches on which they planned to land. US troops landed on Utah and Omaha beaches in the far west, the British on Gold and Sword to the east, with the Canadians sandwiched between the British on Juno.

The Plans

The plan was to capture the beaches then move inland, and capture the Cherbourg port to use as a safe supply harbor. However, bad weather blew many landing crafts off course, while the Americans faced heavy German gunfire on Omaha beach. By midnight on the first day, the Allies had landed most of their forces but failed to achieve many of their objectives.

Landing on Omaha Beach, June 6, 1944

D-Day in numbers

• 5 invasion beaches
• 156,000 total troops landed
• 73,000 American troops landed
• 34,250 most troops landed on a single beach (Omaha)
• 24,000 airborne troops
• 6,939 invasion ships
• 50,000 German defenders
• 10,000 Allied casualties on the first day
• 5,000 German casualties on the first day

FAST FACT!

On the night of the invasion only about 15 percent of Allied paratroopers landed in the right place.

THE LIBERATION OF FRANCE

After the landings on D-Day, the Allies planned to march into central France and toward Paris. However, the Germans defended their occupied territory fiercely. Allied progress was slow until the end of July, when US troops managed to break through the German lines in the far west of Normandy. The Germans were now in full retreat.

The Resistance

The French Resistance played their role in the liberation of France. Before D-Day, they blew up 500 railroad lines, cut telephone cables and destroyed power stations. They also played a part in the liberation of Paris. However, resistance had its costs. After they launched attacks on German troops from the Vercors plateau in the Rhone valley, for example, the Germans sealed the area off and killed 850 people.

Resistance fighters escorting German prisoners during the liberation of Paris.

The Liberation of Paris

On August 19, 1944, Allied troops neared Paris. French Resistance forces in the city rose in revolt, cutting German telephone lines and blowing up supplies of gasoline. Hitler had stated he wanted Paris to be flattened but the Resistance negotiated with the German commander of the city, General von Choltitz, to save the city. On August 25, Free French troops entered Paris. Charles de Gaulle, leader of the Free French, walked down the Champs Elysées, the main street, in triumph. Paris was liberated.

A huge crowd gathers to cheer General de Gaulle at the Place de la Concorde after the liberation of Paris.

A US soldier chats to a group of French children during the Allied campaign to liberate France.

Operation Dragoon

On August 15 1944, Allied troops landed in southern France. Free French troops quickly captured the important ports of Toulon and Marseilles, while US troops chased the Germans up the Rhône valley. By September, they linked up with Allied troops heading east from Normandy.

Operation Market Garden

By September 1944, the Allies had swept across France and liberated Belgium. They now stood on the German frontier. On September 17, British paratroopers attempted to cross the Rhine at Arnhem in the Netherlands and break into Germany itself, but failed. The river was not crossed until the following March, when Allied troops invaded Germany.

FAST FACT!
By 1944, there were around 100,000 Resistance fighters at work throughout France.

PROPAGANDA AND PATRIOTISM

World War II greetings card poking fun at Lord Haw Haw.

Throughout the war, both the Allies and the Axis used propaganda to rally support in their own countries, and to make their enemies fearful. They often exaggerated or stretched the truth to make a point. Propaganda was also used to encourage people to enlist or help with the war effort at home, to sell war bonds, and to boost morale.

Radio

Radio was a powerful medium for spreading propaganda. While both sides used it, two of the most famous radio propaganda stars were on the Axis side. In Japan, there was Tokyo Rose, a female broadcaster who worked at Radio Tokyo. Her show "The Zero Hour" was supposed to insult American troops and lower their morale by giving doctored battle reports, but they listened anyway for the music. Another famous radio host was William Joyce, known as "Lord Haw Haw." He was an American-born British Nazi-sympathizer who'd moved to Berlin and broadcasted pro-German messages in English. After the war, Tokyo Rose was imprisoned, and Lord Haw Haw was hanged.

Stamps

Many countries issued war-themed, patriotic postage stamps to help rally support for their war effort. German stamps featured images of Hitler, soldiers, and weapons. The United States issued the purple 3-cent "Win the War" stamp. It featured an eagle with its wings in the shape of a victory "V" and a banner with the words "Win the War" across its breast.

The patriotic "Win the War" stamp, issued in the US in 1942.

Leaflets

One of the most common ways to spread propaganda was by dropping leaflets on enemy territory. These papers were dropped by the thousands and intended to be picked up by soldiers or ordinary citizens. They offered "news" from the battle front and some encouraged troops to surrender. Others reassured civilians that help was on the way.

Poster promoting the "courageous Russian Army."

"... THE HOPES OF CIVILIZATION REST ON THE WORTHY BANNERS OF THE COURAGEOUS RUSSIAN ARMY." — Gen. Douglas MacArthur

HELP RUSSIAN WAR RELIEF!

EUROPAS FREIHEIT

1941 poster showing a German soldier defeating a red dragon. The dragon represents their enemies: Russia and communism.

NEW WEAPONS

Throughout the war, both sides developed new weapons to use in the conflict. Scientists and inventors devised ingenious new types of bombs, tanks, and guns to attack the enemy. They also came up with simple ideas such as using strips of aluminium to confuse enemy radar.

Perfect Bomber

The American B-17 Flying Fortress bomber was first produced in 1935 but extensively revised in 1941. It could fly higher than any other bomber, thus evading enemy aircraft. It dropped more bombs in the war than any other US bomber.

The V1

In 1942 the Germans developed the V1 flying bomb, known to the Allies as the "doodlebug." This new jet-powered missile could deliver a bomb weighing 1,900 pounds a distance of 150 miles. This early type of missile used a simple autopilot to control its height and speed.

German wartime magazine cover showing a V1 rocket in flight.

Bouncing Bombs

In 1943, British inventor Barnes Wallis invented a round bomb that bounced along the surface of water before hitting its target, thereby avoiding obstacles such as torpedo nets. The bombs were successfully used on May 16–17, 1943, to breach the Möhne and Edersee dams in the Ruhr valley, causing massive floods.

A movie still showing a practice version of the bouncing bomb being tested in Kent.

The World's First Rocket

The German V2 rocket was developed in 1944. It was the world's first long-range ballistic missile and forerunner of the space rocket. It could fire a 2,200-pound warhead a distance of 200 miles. Both the V1 and V2 caused immense damage in London and Antwerp in the last year of the war.

A Flying Fortress bomber leaving Langley Field in Virginia, USA.

Chaff

In order to confuse the enemy's radar, the British, Americans, and Germans all dropped small, thin strips of aluminum, metallized glass fiber, or plastic (chaff) over bomb targets. This filled up the radar screens and made it impossible for the enemy to distinguish it from incoming aircraft.

Guns and Tanks

Both sides developed new guns and tanks. The Germans went one better by developing panzerjäger or tank-hunters, which were armored vehicles specially equipped with powerful guns to hunt down and knock out enemy tanks.

103

THE PLOT AGAINST HITLER

Hermann Göring (center) showing officials the wreckage following the failed July bomb plot to assassinate Hitler.

There were plenty of Germans who disapproved of Adolf Hitler's policies and felt strongly that he needed to be eliminated. Hitler was the target of more than thirty assassination attempts over the years. The one that came closest to succeeding, known as the July Plot or Operation Valkyrie, took place on July 20, 1944.

Claus von Stauffenberg.

Colonel von Stauffenberg

The man behind the assassination attempt was Colonel Claus von Stauffenberg. Stauffenberg was a 36-year-old military officer who'd lost an eye and a hand in North Africa. Even before that had happened, he'd decided to try to overthrow Hitler, and worked with others to organize a coup.

The Original Plan

According to the original plan, Hitler and his two top men, Göring and Himmler, were to be killed at the same time. A group of conspirators would then seize control of the government.

What Actually Happened

Von Stauffenberg arrived at Hitler's headquarters in Rastenberg, East Prussia, where Hitler was having a meeting with senior officials. He was carrying a briefcase containing a bomb. Stauffenberg sat down, placed the briefcase on the floor, and pushed it with his foot closer to Hitler. He then left the room saying he had to make a phone call. Five minutes later, the bomb exploded. Four men died, but Hitler survived. His right arm and shoulder were injured, but he was otherwise okay.

The Aftermath

After the unsuccessful attempt, the main perpetrators were not the only ones executed. Hitler had almost 5,000 additional opponents rounded up and killed.

Claus von Stauffenberg's brother, Berthold, was tried and executed for his part in the plot.

FAST FACT!

Noted general Erwin Rommel was implicated in the assassination plot and forced by Hitler to commit suicide.

OPERATION BAGRATION

After their successes at Stalingrad and Kursk in 1943, the Soviet Red Army slowly pushed the Germans out of central Russia. The next year, they initiated Operation Bagration to clear the Germans out of western Russia. By the end of August 1944, the Russians had inflicted a massive defeat on the Germans.

Soviet troops cross a pontoon bridge at the Western Bug River, July 1944.

FAST FACT!

Nearly 80,0000 Poles took part in Operation Bagration.

Prince Pyotr Bagration.

Who was Bagration?

Prince Pyotr Bagration was a hero of Russian history. He was a general in the Imperial Russian Army during the war with Napoleon of France in the early 1800s. His name was chosen for this new offensive against the Germans to inspire the Red Army.

Timing is Everything

Operation Bagration was launched just two weeks after D-Day, causing an Axis crisis on two fronts at the same time. It was the beginning of the end for Germany.

"Maskirovka"

Maskirovka is Russian for "deception." The Russians used maskirovka to deceive the Germans into expecting a Russian offensive in the Ukraine. The main Russian attack actually took place to the north in Belarus. The Germans were caught by surprise and many of their troops were surrounded. By the end of the campaign, the Russians were within striking distance of Berlin.

To show the world the scale of the Soviet victory, 50,000 German PoWs were paraded through Moscow in July, 1944.

Bagration in Numbers

- 381,000 Germans killed
- 158,480 Germans captured
- 180,040 Russians killed
- 590,848 Russians wounded

Warsaw Uprising

As the Red Army approached the Polish capital, Warsaw, the Polish resistance Home Army rose in revolt on August 1, 1944. They intended to liberate their city from Nazi rule before the Soviets arrived. The Germans crushed the uprising by October 2, with a huge loss of Polish life. Almost 180,000 people died during the Warsaw Uprising, including 20,000 Home Army soldiers.

Warsaw in ruins.

LIBERATING THE JEWS

The advance of the Allies had caused deportations to Nazi concentration camps to all but cease by the end of 1944. However, the deaths continued. As the Allied troops approached in the months that followed, some camps were abandoned, and their inmates forced to make long marches to other camps away from the front lines. The end for the Germans was inevitable. One by one, concentration camps throughout the former Axis territory were liberated.

Some of the thousands of wedding rings the Nazis removed from their victims to salvage the gold.

A Terrible Sight

Allied troops moving through central and eastern Europe knew almost nothing about Nazi concentration camps. As they arrived at the camps, they were met with unimaginable horrors. Alongside the thousands of terribly thin and sick inmates, there were huge piles of dead bodies.

Survivors from Dachau concentration camp celebrate their freedom, April 1945.

FAST FACT!

The Italian chemist and later author Primo Levi took nine months to get home after being freed.

Getting Home

Freedom was not the end for the Jews. Many were extremely weak and needed medical care. Once they were stronger, they had to figure out how to get back to their homes, which were often many hundreds of miles away. Not only that, they had no idea what would greet them when they arrived. Were any of their family members or friends still alive?

Nuremberg Trials

In August 1945, an International Military Tribunal was formed to prosecute major Nazi war criminals who had committed crimes against humanity, among other things. Twenty-two Nazis were tried in Nuremberg, Germany, in 1945–46. On October 1, 1946, the verdicts were announced: twelve Nazis were sentenced to death, three received life in prison, and four received a sentence of between 10–20 years in prison. Three were acquitted.

V-MAIL

During the war, the only way soldiers could keep in touch with their loved ones was through letters. Wartime letters were written on special forms called V-Mail. Delivery time overseas could take anywhere from five days to more than two weeks, especially around Christmas time.

Letters Home

Starting in March 1942, soldiers were allowed to send letters for free. To make delivery of letters to and from soldiers more efficient, an ingenious system was introduced in June 1942. After writing your letter on a Victory Mail (V-Mail for short) form, the letter was microfilmed for more efficient shipping. Once overseas, they were printed and delivered.

Microfilm is a reel of film on which printed materials are photographed at greatly reduced size for ease of storage.

Space Saver

Between 1,500 and 1,800 V-Mail letters could fit on one roll of film, saving a tremendous amount of space. 150,000 ordinary letters would weigh 2,575 pounds and take up 37 mail sacks. 150,000 microfilmed V-mail letters weighed 45 pounds and fit in one mail sack. In its first two years, V-Mail saved about 4,964,286 cargo pounds, enough to ship 496,428 rifles or 1,323,809 units of blood plasma.

Hard at work inside the V-Mail room at the Pentagon, Washington, D.C.

A courier delivering letters ready for sorting and photographing.

FAST FACT!

By 1945 a total of 2,533,938,330 letters had been sent to Army personnel!

Censored!

Every V-Mail letter was carefully read by censors to make sure that no sensitive information was leaked—such as a soldier's exact location or anything to do with weapons or strategy. Anything questionable that was found would be crossed out in black.

BATTLE OF THE BULGE

By December 1944, the Allies had pushed the Germans out of France, Belgium, and the southern Netherlands. They were ready to cross the Rhine and attack Germany. But all of a sudden, the Germans launched a massive offensive in the forested Ardennes region of eastern Belgium that caught the Allies totally by surprise. It was the last German offensive of the war. After this point, they would be strictly on the retreat.

FAST FACT!
The Germans later named the attack Operation Mist, because it took place in misted forests.

The German Plan

The Germans planned to strike a weakly defended section of Allied-controlled territory in the Ardennes. They would then head northwest to recapture the important port of Antwerp. In so doing, they hoped to split the Allied front line in half and surround many of its larger divisions, forcing the Allies to make peace.

Different Names

The Germans called the battle the Unternehmen Wacht am Rhein ("Operation Watch on the Rhine"), the French called it the Bataille des Ardennes ("Battle of the Ardennes"). The British and Americans called it the Ardennes Counteroffensive, but it was the name the newspapers gave it that stuck. The German attack created a huge bulge in the Allied lines, hence the name Battle of the Bulge.

The Campaign

On December 16, 1944, overcast weather kept Allied planes grounded. The Germans took advantage and attacked the Allies, creating a big bulge in their front line 70 miles deep. Eventually, the Germans ran out of fuel and other supplies, and by January 25, 1945, they were forced back through the forest.

Two German foot soldiers pass by a burning tank during the Battle of the Bulge.

American soldier in the town of St Vith during the Ardennes Offensive.

Bulge in Numbers

- American troops: 505,000
- British troops: 55,000
- German troops: 600,000
- Allied casualties: 75,000
- Axis casualties: 100,000
- Tanks lost: 800+ on both sides

THE SIEGE OF BUDAPEST

As the Russians advanced from the east, the Germans fought desperately to repel them and protect Axis territory. By December of 1944, the Hungarian capital city of Budapest was in danger of being lost. Hitler viewed the city as an essential stronghold, and ordered its defense. From December 1944 to February 1945, the city was a war zone.

The Plan of Attack

The Russians pushed from two fronts, through the flat suburbs of Pest on the east bank of the Danube River and through the hills of Buda on the west bank of the Danube. Bombs and mortars damaged many buildings around the city.

Budapest residents clearing up the city streets after the battles.

Life Under Siege

Food was scarce that winter and some resorted to eating horse meat. Apartment building windows were blown out by bombs, and heat was hard to come by. Meanwhile, the Russians continued their attack. On December 25, they took 2,300 prisoners in Budapest and by the end of that month they had the city completely surrounded. January of 1945 saw some of the fiercest fighting of the whole war. It was very dangerous to set foot outside during this time.

FAST FACT!

During and after the siege, Russian troops looted the city of Budapest.

Retreat

On January 18, the Germans were forced to retreat west across the Danube River from Pest to Buda. The fighting went on in Buda until early February. Since the defense of the city was hopeless, the remaining soldiers were ordered to retreat. Of the 30,000 Axis soldiers who tried to escape, fewer than 1,000 made it back to safety. In total, 122,000 troops and 38,000 civilians were killed during the siege.

PRISONERS OF WAR

Allied troops fighting on the front lines were always at risk of being captured by the enemy, as were pilots whose planes were shot down over enemy territory. Though Germany had signed the Geneva Convention in 1929, which set guidelines for the humane treatment of prisoners of war, conditions in many of the German prison camps were poor.

"Being a prisoner of war is a grim business. You live behind barbed wire, under constant guard . . . From the moment you are captured you have certain rights . . . Stand up for your rights, but do it with military courtesy and firmness at all times. The enemy will respect you for it."

—US War Department, May 1944

Being Prepared

In May 1944, The US War Department issued a 19-page pamphlet titled "If You Should be Captured These Are Your Rights." This booklet explained what to expect as a prisoner of war.

FAST FACT!

Allied troops captured during the fighting in Europe were often shipped to Germany crammed in railroad boxcars.

Getting the News

Often, the first sign of trouble a family member received was an unopened, returned letter marked "Missing." This unsettling piece of mail might be the only information available for months, until official word arrived explaining that their loved one had been taken prisoner.

The Great Escape

On the night of March 24, 1944,
76 British and Commonwealth prisoners attempted a
daring escape from Stalag Luft III German prison camp
through a 330-foot tunnel they'd dug. Only 3 reached
safety. Of the 73 recaptured, 50 were executed.

Japanese Conditions

Japan had not signed the Geneva Convention and conditions
in their camps were worse than German ones. Out of 5,436
US Army Air Force personnel captured by the Japanese during
the war, only 2,879 (53 percent) were still alive by the end
of the war. More than 650 had been killed trying to
escape, and 1,847 had died in captivity.

RAF pilots at Stalag
Luft III, the scene
of the most daring
escape attempted
by POWs in WWII

117

1945: WAR ENDS

At the start of 1945, it was clear that the war with Germany was in its final few months. Allied armies attacked the country from either side as they headed to the capital, Berlin. But the war against Japan threatened to continue for some years, because the Japanese fiercely defended their territory. Only the use of a terrifying new weapon brought the world war to an end.

The Russian flag being raised atop the Reichtsag in Berlin, 1945.

Key Events

FEBRUARY 11
Red Army takes Budapest in Hungary.

MARCH 7
Allies cross undefended bridge over the Rhine at Remagen.

MARCH 26
US troops capture Iwo Jima (see page 128).

APRIL 12
Roosevelt dies and is succeeded by Harry Truman.

APRIL 25
Red Army surrounds Berlin.

KEY

	Axis and Axis-held (May 1945)
	Allies and Allies-held (May 1945)
	Neutral nations
→	Main lines of Axis advance
→	Main lines of Allied advance
⇢	Allied amphibious landings
—	Axis frontline
☀1	Manila
☀2	Iwo Jima
☀3	Okinawa
☀4	Hiroshima
☀5	Nagasaki

USSR

MONGOLIA

MANCHUKO (Japan)

AFGHANISTAN

CHINA

KOREA (Japan)

JAPAN

INDIA (Britain)

BURMA (U.K.)

Bay of Bengal

Arabian Sea

CEYLON (Britain)

SIAM

FRENCH INDO-CHINA

PHILIPPINES

BRITISH MALAYA

DUTCH EAST INDIES

INDIAN OCEAN

GUAM (USA)

CAROLINE ISLANDS (Japan)

MARSHALL ISLANDS (Japan)

PACIFIC OCEAN

ALASKA (USA)

HAWAIIAN ISLANDS (USA)

NORTHEAST NEW GUINEA

PAPUA (Australia)

SOLOMON ISLANDS (Britain)

NEW HEBRIDES (France/Britain)

NEW CALEDONIA (France)

SAMOA

FIJI (Britain)

AUSTRALIA

NEW ZEALAND

FAST FACT!

The Germans surrended twice—in Reims, France, on May 7, and in Berlin on May 8.

APRIL 28
Mussolini killed by partisans.

APRIL 30
Hitler commits suicide (see page 122).

MAY 7
German High Command surrenders unconditionally.

AUGUST 6, 9
Atomic bombs dropped on Japan (see page 132).

AUGUST 14
Japan surrenders (see page 134).

THE INVASION OF GERMANY

At the start of 1945, the Allies stood poised on the borders of Germany—The Americans and British by the River Rhine in the west and the Russians on the border with German Prussia to the east. The next four months were to see some of the most brutal and desperate fighting of the war as the Allies closed in on the capital of Berlin from both sides.

Winston Churchill crosses the Rhine with US and British generals on March 25, 1945.

Western Front

After the failure of the Ardennes offensive, Germany lacked strength in the west. On March 7, the Americans seized an undefended bridge across the Rhine at Remagen. On March 22, they crossed the Rhine in assault boats. The Germans were forced to fall back. The Allies poured into central Germany and encircled the industrial area of the Ruhr, along with the 325,000 German troops that were defending it. These Germans were taken prisoner, drastically weakening the Nazis.

The Eastern Front—North

In January 1945, two vast Russian armies moved into Poland and eastern Germany on their way to Berlin. Warsaw fell to the Russians on January 17. By February 3, the 1st Byelorussian Front army had crossed the River Oder, only 40 miles from Berlin. On April 25, Berlin was surrounded by Russian troops.

The Eastern Front—South

Russian troops occupied Romania and Bulgaria in August and September 1944. They then swept north into Hungary, seizing its capital Budapest in February 1945. The British had already liberated Greece and partisans had liberated Yugoslavia and Albania. The Balkans were now free from German rule.

Prisoners carrying their wounded on stretchers, Remagen, Germany, March 1945.

Soviet signalers advancing into the city of Berlin, 1945.

Battle of Berlin

On March 31, 1945, Stalin ordered the Soviet army to continue to push forward toward Berlin. By April 16, Russian troops were in position just 40 miles outside of Berlin. By the 21st, they had reached the German outer defensive ring around the city and were poised to strike.

THE DEATH OF HITLER

With the Russian army surrounding Berlin, Hitler was trapped. He spent his last days in his underground bunker issuing orders to nonexistent armies. His campaign of world domination was over.

Berlin 1945, cleaning up the rubble of the bombed-out city.

US soldiers learn of Hitler's death.

Hitler's Death

On April 29, 1945, Adolf Hitler married his long-term girlfriend, Eva Braun. A day later, he shot himself in his underground bunker in Berlin. Eva Braun took a cyanide pill and also died. Following Hitler's orders, his body was doused in gasoline and set alight in the Reich Chancellery garden.

Final Days

After the Russians surrounded Berlin on April 25, their artillery pounded the city. The next day, half a million troops poured in. On April 30, two Russian sergeants broke into the Reichstag, seat of the German government. That evening they raised the Red Flag over the building. The remaining German troops finally surrendered to the Russians on May 2.

The German Surrender

There was absolutely no hope left for German victory. It was over. On May 7, the German general Alfred Jodl unconditionally surrendered all remaining German forces to the Allies at Reims, France. On May 9, Field Marshal Wilhelm Keitel signed a similar document with the Russians in Berlin.

V-E Day

Victory in Europe Day was celebrated on May 8, 1945. A struggle that had lasted almost six years was finally over. While there was much joy at the defeat of the Axis powers in Europe, the Allies could not rest easy yet. The war with Japan still raged on.

Victory in Europe celebrations in Bristol, England. Street parties took place all over Europe and America.

123

THE MERKERS TREASURE

On April 6, 1945, American military police in the town of Merkers (200 miles south of Berlin) came across two women who were suspiciously out after curfew. The women were questioned and before long, they revealed that the nearby Kaiseroda Salt Mine was actually a Nazi hiding place for gold and other valuables. The Americans went to investigate.

FAST FACT!

As late as 1997, there were still over 5 tons of Merkers gold that had yet to be returned to its rightful owners.

US commanders tour the salt mine where Nazi treasure was hidden.

In the Mine

Seeing that the vault door was locked, they used dynamite to blast a hole in the brick vault wall. Inside they found an incredible fortune in money and precious metals, including rings and gold fillings from Holocaust victims, and gold from banks in occupied countries.

Stolen masterpiece found in Germany at the end of the war.

Artwork Too

As well as precious metals and currency, there was a treasure trove of valuable works of art, sculptures, antique rugs, and tapestries. All were in danger of damage and had to be carefully transported out of the mine.

Reichsbank gold, SS loot, and paintings in Merkers salt mine, April 15, 1945.

Hidden in the Dough

There were many other instances of Nazis trying to hide valuables from the Allies. Besides mines, they chose other seemingly innocent places. In the town of Ash, an SS officer had actually baked precious stones and jewelry into 60 loaves of bread. American soldiers dining at the SS officer's house noticed the loaves and thought they were suspicious. Further investigation revealed the loot.

The Merkers Treasure

- 3,682 bags of German currency containing 2.76 billion marks
- 8,307 gold bars
- 55 boxes of gold bullion
- 3,326 bags of German, British, American, and French gold coins
- 63 bags of silver
- 8 bags of gold rings

Total value over $520 million

125

TRUMAN TAKES OVER

By early 1945, the strain of the war had taken its toll on President Roosevelt. He had a weak heart and high blood pressure. He suffered from a bad cold, and his trip to the Big Three conference at Yalta did not help his health. Roosevelt arrived at his second home in Warm Springs, Georgia, in early April 1945, thinking the fresh air would help him. He died on the afternoon of April 12 of a cerebral hemorrhage.

Franklin Roosevelt, the 32nd President of the United States (1933–45).

FAST FACT!

Harry S. Truman had only been vice president for two months and 23 days when he became president.

Unconditional Surrender

Thousands of people line the streets during Roosevelt's funeral procession in Washington, D.C.

Two hours after the death of Roosevelt, Vice President Harry Truman was sworn in as the next American president. In his first speech as president, on April 16, 1945, Truman laid out his plans to win the war:

"America will continue the fight for freedom until no vestige of resistance remains! . . . America will never become a party to any plan for partial victory! To settle for merely another temporary respite would surely jeopardize the future security of all the world. Our demand has been, and it remains— Unconditional Surrender!"

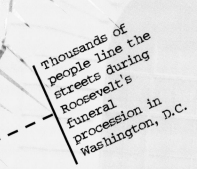

Harry S. Truman, the 33rd President of the United States (1945–53).

Term Limits

After Roosevelt's death, there was a push for presidential term limits. Congress passed the 22nd Amendment to the Constitution in 1947, and it was ratified in 1951. It stated that a president could not serve more than two terms in office.

127

IWO JIMA AND OKINAWA

In 1944–45, American troops moved island-by-island closer to Japan. They gained naval bases in the Philippines and air bases in Iwo Jima and Okinawa. By now they could inflict huge damage on Japan itself, but it was clear that an invasion would be very costly to human life.

US planes prepare for take off against the Japanese forces in Manila.

The Philippines

On October 17, 1944, American troops attacked the Philippine Islands, defeating a 67-ship-strong Japanese fleet in the Leyte Gulf by October 27. In February, they captured the main island of Luzon and the capital, Manila, suffering 146,000 casualties. Japanese troops retreated to the hills and continued to fight on.

Burma

After the Japanese invaded British Burma in January 1942, a largely forgotten war began. Up to one million British troops, mostly drawn from India, fought the Japanese in the hot jungle. In 1944, the Japanese invaded India but were defeated at Kohima and Imphal. By May 1945, the Allies had reconquered most of Burma.

British soldiers in the Burmese jungle.

The Islands

The Americans needed air bases from which to hit Japan. On February 15, 1945, they attacked the small island of Iwo Jima, encountering fierce resistance there. On April 1, 1945, American troops landed at Okinawa, southwest of Japan. American ships fired nearly 100,000 shells and rockets on the Japanese garrisons. More than 150,000 Japanese soldiers and civilians died before the Americans finally seized control on June 30.

Two Notable Deaths

The highest-ranking US officer to be killed during the war was General Simon Buckner, who was hit by shell fire while visiting the front line troops on Okinawa on June 18. The popular war reporter Ernie Pyle was killed on April 18 by enemy fire on a small island off the coast of Okinawa.

FAST FACT!

27 Medals of Honor were awarded to those fighting on Iwo Jima, more than any other battle in American history.

ATTACKING JAPAN

Now that the United States had won victories on islands very near to Japan, it had air bases within striking range. Bombing runs could now inflict heavy damage directly on Japanese cities. It helped that the Americans had thousands of B-29 long-range Superfortress bombers to use for these missions.

Truly a Superfortress

The Superfortress could carry double the bombs of the Boeing B-17 Flying Fortress. At 99 feet long, the Superfortress was a giant among warplanes, and could fly long distances from US bases in the Mariana Islands because of their huge fuel tanks.

American B—29 Super Fortress bomber over Japan, 1945. The smoke below shows where the bombs hit.

FAST FACT!

By April 1945, plans were being made for "Downfall," a full-scale invasion of Japan.

Bombs Away

- May 14: 500 bombers drop over a million firebombs on the city of Nagoya.
- May 17: 500 planes leave the city of Nagoya in flames.
- May 24: 550 bombers dropped 750,000 bombs on industrial sites in Tokyo.
- June 1: 600 planes drop 3,200 tons of bombs over Osaka.
- June 6: the city of Kobe is hit by 3,000 tons of fire bombs.

Relentless Raids

As spring turned to summer, the bombing raids continued to inflict major damage on Japanese cities. Toyama was 95 percent destroyed, Nagaoka 65 percent destroyed, Mito 61 percent destroyed, and Hachioji 56 percent destroyed.

Any End in Sight?

Millions of Japanese fled from their home cities into the countryside. Food was rationed and morale was falling. But was it enough? How much bombing would it take to force Japan to surrender? American military leaders were unsure.

Demolished buildings after a bombing raid, Tokyo, 1945.

THE ATOMIC BOMB

At the Potsdam Conference in the ruins of Berlin on July 26 1945, the United States, Britain and China called for Japan to surrender or face "prompt and utter destruction." This demand was delivered on August 6th and 9th, when the world's first atomic bombs were dropped on Hiroshima and Nagasaki.

A mushroom cloud formed by an atomic bomb in Hiroshima.

The aftermath of the Hiroshima atomic bomb.

The Manhattan Project

In 1942, American and British scientists began to develop atomic weapons in a project known as the Manhattan Project. By 1945, they had produced three bombs. The first one was tested successfully in the desert of New Mexico on July 16, 1945. Secrecy was so critical to the success of the Manhattan Project that many scientists employed by the government didn't even know what it was that they had been working on until after the atomic bombs were dropped.

Bombing Japan

The world's second atomic bomb, a uranium device called "Little Boy," was dropped on Hiroshima on August 6th. Three days later, a plutonium bomb called "Fat Man," was to be dropped on Kokura. However, the city was covered with smoke after a bombing raid so Nagasaki was hit instead.

The Effects

Within four months of the two bombings, up to 160,000 people in Hiroshima and 80,000 in Nagasaki were dead. Most of the deaths occurred within the first 24 hours, but thousands more died of radiation sickness, burns, and other injuries. The centers of both cities were reduced to ashes.

Mother and child in Hiroshima, December 1945, four months after the atomic bomb dropped.

JAPAN SURRENDERS

During the summer of 1945, Japanese cities came under constant bombardment from American bombers. After the United States dropped the atomic bombs and the USSR declared war and invaded Japanese-held territory, Japan had no choice but to surrender.

The End of the War

Japanese surrender was announced on August 15, 1945, which became known as V-J Day (Victory over Japan). Japanese officials signed the formal Japanese Instrument of Surrender aboard USS *Missouri* on September 2, and that, too has been referred to as V-J Day.

Cheering crowds in Times Square on V–J Day, after the announcement of the Japanese surrender.

Occupied Japan

On August 28, 1945, General Douglas MacArthur, Supreme Commander of the Allied Powers, began the Allied occupation of Japan. Hundreds of thousands of American troops occupied Japan between 1945 and 1951, with the stated goal, approved by President Truman, of turning Japan into a disarmed, peaceful, free nation.

"This is the day we have been waiting for since Pearl Harbor. This is the day when Fascism finally dies, as we always knew it would."

—President Truman, August 15, 1945

Fighting On

Many Japanese soldiers refused to surrender and fought on in isolated islands and jungle retreats. The last Japanese soldiers, known as "holdouts," did not surrender until 1974, one in the Philippines and one in Indonesia.

Japanese officers surrender their swords to British soldiers at the end of the war.

The Japanese surrender at Tokyo Bay, Japan on September 2, 1945.

THE COST OF WAR

The cost of World War II was immense. Millions were dead, thousands of towns and cities destroyed, train lines and roads blown up, and basic services like electricity and water unavailable. Of course, the greatest cost was paid by those who lost their lives, and those who lost family and friends.

A makeshift headstone marks the location of an American soldier killed during the Normandy invasion.

Casualties

COUNTRY	DIED	PERCENTAGE POPULATION
Poland	5,820,000	16.7%
USSR	26,600,000	13.5%
Germany	6,900,000	10%
Japan	3,120,000	4.37%
China	20,000,000	3.86%
France	550,000	1.35%
Italy	454,600	1.03%
Britain	450,900	0.94%
USA	420,000	0.32%

The Human Cost

It is difficult to calculate the total number of people who died during the war, but it is estimated to be around 60 million: 38 million civilians and 22 million military personnel. A further 25 million people died from war-related diseases and famine. On average 30,000 people were killed every day.

The Financial Cost

The amount of money spent on the war was astronomical. The United States' military spending was $296 billion, which today would be more than $4 trillion. It amounted to 36 percent of the value of the Gross Domestic Product, which is the term for everything the country produced during those four years.

Arlington National Cemetery, Washington D.C.

Physical Damage

Bombing raids caused immense damage throughout Europe. Some German cities, such as Dresden, were completely flattened by bombs, and many other large European cities were severely damaged. For example, 85 percent of Warsaw (Poland) was destroyed and in Salzburg, Austria, 46 percent of the city's buildings were destroyed. American attacks on Japan destroyed 2.5 million houses and 40 percent of the major cities.

Two elderly German men sitting on a crate amid the rubble of bombed Berlin, 1945.

THE POST-WAR WORLD

The world we live in today evolved out of reactions to the war. Organizations such as the United Nations, the North Atlantic Treaty Organization (NATO), and the European Union owe their birth to the war, as do many of the world's financial and trading institutions. Many countries set up welfare systems for their people, such as the National Health Service in Britain, as a response to the war.

Between 1961 and 1989 a wall divided the German city of Berlin in two.

A Divided World

After the war, Russian troops occupied eastern Europe and American troops occupied western Europe. Germany was divided between them. The division soon became permanent. An **"Iron Curtain"** across Europe separated the two sides as the communist USSR and democratic US became bitter rivals in what became known as the Cold War. Europe remained divided until the collapse of Communism in 1989 and the reunification of Germany in 1990.

The United Nations

On December 29, 1941, US President Roosevelt and British Prime Minister Churchill drafted a Declaration of the United Nations in which they pledged to support principles such as life, liberty, and independence in the fight against the Axis. By the end of the war, 45 more nations had signed the declaration. These nations formed the membership of a permanent United Nations organization that came into operation in 1945.

The United Nations Secretariat Building in New York City.

The European Union

World War II was the third time in 70 years that France and Germany had fought each other. After the war, politicians from both countries decided to make sure it did not happen again. This led to the signing of the Treaty of Rome in 1957, that created a European Economic Community, the forerunner of the 28-member European Union that exists today. The various treaties have kept western Europe at peace since 1945, the longest period of peace in its history.

The European Union flag represents the unity of the countries of the Union.

WHO'S WHO?

Clement Attlee

1883–1967
British prime minister during the last months of the war in 1945 until 1951.

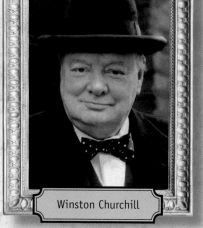

Winston Churchill

1874–1965
War time prime minister of Britain from 1940–45, prime minster again from 1951–55.

Dwight D. Eisenhower

1890–1969
Supreme Allied Commander in Europe (1943–45), and the 34th President of the United States.

General Charles de Gaulle

1890–1970
Leader of the Free French from 1940 and president of liberated France from 1944–46, prime minister then president from 1958–69.

Field Marshal Sir Bernard Montgomery

1887–1978
Commander of the British 8th Army at El-Alamein, October 1942 and commander of Allied ground forces following D-Day in June 1944.

Franklin D. Roosevelt

1882–1945
American president from 1933 throughout the war up to his death in April 1945.

Joseph Stalin

1878–1953
Leader of the USSR from the mid-1920s until his death in 1953.

Harry Truman

1884–1972
American president from the last months of the war in 1945 until 1953.

General Georgy Zhukov

1896–1974
Organizer of the resistance in Leningrad to the German siege, defender of Moscow, victor at Stalingrad and Kursk, one of the leaders of the Red Army that entered Berlin to end the war in May 1945.

Joseph Goebbels

1897–1945
Nazi Minister of Propaganda from 1933–45 and close friend and associate of Hitler.

Hermann Göring

1893–1946
Founder of the Gestapo, Commander-in-Chief of the Luftwaffe and designated successor to Hitler.

Reinhard Heydrich

1904–1942
High-ranking Nazi and chair of the Wannsee Conference of 1942 that organized the "Final Solution" to the "Jewish problem."

Heinrich Himmler

1900–45
Leading Nazi, head of the SS from 1929–45, and the man most responsible for the Holocaust.

Emperor Hirohito

1901–1989
Emperor of Japan from 1926 until his death in 1989.

Adolf Hitler

1889–1945
Leader of the Nazi Party from 1921, Führer or leader of Germany from 1933 until his death in 1945.

Benito Mussolini

1883–1945
Leader of Fascist Italy from 1922 to 1943. Known as Il Duce ('the leader'), he was executed by partisans in 1945.

General Erwin Rommel

1891–1944
Highly decorated World War I officer and leader of the Panzer Army in Africa 1941–43. Accused of being involved in a conspiracy to assassinate Hitler in 1944.

Hideki Tojo

1884–1948
Prime Minister of Japan from 1941–44, responsible for taking Japan into the war.

GLOSSARY

Allies, the
Britain and Commonwealth countries, France, the USA, the USSR and others that fought the Axis nations during the war.

Annexation
The forcible taking by one country of another country's territory.

Axis, the
Germany, Italy, Japan, and their allies.

Big Three, the
Winston Churchill, prime minister of Britain, Franklin D. Roosevelt, president of the USA, and Joseph Stalin, leader of the USSR.

Blitzkrieg
German term meaning "lightning war," used to describe a rapid form of warfare using tanks and other armored vehicles, supported by aircraft. The British later shortened the term to "Blitz" to describe the German bombing of their cities.

Collaboration
Working with and supporting an enemy occupier of your country.

Colony
Region or country controlled by another country as part of its empire.

Communism
Belief in a society in which everyone is equal and all property is owned by the state.

Convoy
Fleet of merchant ships escorted by armed warships to protect them from attack.

Democracy
Government by the people or their elected representatives.

Dictatorship
Country governed by a leader who has complete control and often rules by force.

Empire
Group of different nations and peoples ruled by one nation and its emperor.

Fascism
Extreme political movement founded in Italy based on nationalism and strong government.

Free France
Movement set up in 1940 by General de Gaulle in exile in London to liberate France from German rule.

Führer
German word for "leader," used as a title by Adolf Hitler.

Ghetto
City districts set up by the Nazi regime in order to segregate Jews, and other minority groups. Conditions in the ghettos were very poor.

Guerrilla
(Member of) a group of soldiers taking part in unofficial fighting against an occupying country's armies.

Holocaust, the
Attempt by the Nazis to murder all the Jews in Europe.

Incendiary bomb
Bomb designed to cause fires.

Iron Curtain
Fortified border that ran across Europe between the Communist east and the democratic west; it was torn down after the collapse of Communism in 1990.

Nationalism
Strong belief in and support of one's own country.

Nazi
Member of the National Socialist German Workers' Party, led by Adolf Hitler, which held extreme racist and authoritarian views.

Neutral
Country that refuses to take sides in a war and does not fight.

Pact
Formal agreement between two or more countries.

Partisan
Member of an armed resistance group fighting inside a country against an invading or occupying army.

Rearmament
Building up a new supply of weapons.

Red Army
The army of the USSR.

Third Reich
Third German Reich or Empire, led by Adolf Hitler.

Treaty of Versailles
Treaty signed in 1919 in Paris that ended the First World War.

U-boat
Unterseeboot, or "undersea boat," a German submarine.

Unconditional surrender
To surrender without any conditions attached.

USSR
Union of the Soviet Socialist Republics, or Soviet Russia, a communist state.

Vichy France
Government of France after its defeat by Germany in 1940; nominally in charge of the whole country but in effect only in full control of unoccupied southern France; Vichy France was occupied by the Germans in November 1942 and then existed in name only for the rest of the war.

INDEX